The
SHOULDING

A Story of Resilience and Hope

By Roberta Brown

PAGE PUBLISHING, INC.
New York, NY

SPOTLIGHT PUBLISHING
Goodyear, AZ

First originally published by Page Publishing, Inc. 2016
Second publishing - Spotlight Publishing - 2020

ISBN 978-1-7354690-4-1(2020)
ISBN 978-1-68348-025-9 (pbk)
ISBN 978-1-68348-026-6 (digital)

Printed in the United States of America

and visit relatives. In writing it down it all seems a bit benign. We had chalk portraits done at Disneyland. My sister laughed as she was making me sick on the Teacup Ride. The sicker I got, the harder she laughed. The rest are just memories through pictures.

We took fishing trips up north to Brainerd, Gull Lake, and Eshquaguma. I swam, I skied, I played tennis. I was the closest thing to a jock my dad would have. He always wanted boys, but no such luck. That didn't stop him from letting us know how we fell short in that department. I know that writing my story is going to open up a lot of pain for me, but I'm hoping it will be a healing, cathartic experience.

How do we know that we are living in a "normal" family? Who defines "normal?" As I said, growing up there was a lot of yelling, a lot of fighting. As time went on, fighting became emotional and physical abuse from my father—my mother's role in this I didn't really realize until I was fifty-one.

Time to take a deep, cleansing breath…

My really early memories of abuse were being slapped in the face, in the head, and spanked on my behind. I only recall a specific spanking when I was seven or eight after accidentally breaking a floodlight at a neighbor's pond. I was so afraid to own up to it, and when I did, I was spanked and told I would have to pay for the floodlight and apologize to the neighbors. I was grounded as well. Pretty harsh for an accident. That was a theme in our house.

Early on I was labeled as "stupid, careless, and lazy." I don't know why. I was never any of those things. But that was a constant. I accidentally broke a dish from a set of Royal Doulton china my parents brought back from England. All hell broke loose. Not only was I stupid, careless, and lazy, I was going to pay for being all of those things. I had to order a replacement dish and go pay for it. Mind you, this was not like a Greek wedding where people break plates on purpose, it was an accident. Oh, I was grounded after that too. I started becoming afraid to touch any material thing that belonged to my parents.

When I was sixteen, my parents went on vacation and left me alone for the first time. As any sixteen-year-old I planned to have a party. I called this the "don't break the yellow lamp" party. Only my

CHAPTER 2

OCD, PTSD
and Other Disorders

PTSD—posttraumatic stress disorder. That happens to war veterans, right? I remember hearing about PTSD in association with the Vietnam War. Never in a million years did I think PTSD would be a big part of my life. PTSD for me rears its ugly head in many different ways. Sometimes I split right out of my body and view things from above where the things are happening to me. Sometimes it's ringing in my ears; sometimes it's no ringing at all. Sometimes I go blank and sit as time passes. Sometimes I go blank, continue doing tasks, "come to," and it's been several hours. Things are put away, laundry is done, drawers and closets organized, and I have no recollection. If I have to choose one, the blanking out and getting stuff done would be my preference, although the "losing time" part doesn't sit too well with me. It has never happened while I'm driving myself around. I know that if something has got me really upset, I would call my best friend and have her talk to me to keep me centered. Other PTSD symptoms would be uncontrollable shaking and crying and/or not being able to sleep. It all depends on what the trigger is.

being in control of my destiny or destination. I can only remember that kind of PTSD event happening that one time.

I have always had a certain amount of anxiety for as long as I remember. I knew as a little girl, going to school was hard. My mom would walk me to the bus stop, and I would cry when I had to get on the bus. Whether that was separation anxiety or fear of what unknown thing was going to happen at school, I was not sure. But again, I was afraid of everything all of the time.

There have been some more recent out-of-body PTSD events. I think it was three years ago at another "lovely," dysfunctional Thanksgiving dinner at my sister's. Things had gone pretty smoothly. No fighting, not much belittling, probably because my sister had invited some friends of hers to join us. So I would say best behavior was being displayed. I was all for it! As usual, after dinner, I was clearing plates and cleaning up. I went back to the table to take a plate from my niece, and she and my dad were in some kind of deep discussion. As I walked up I heard my dad say to her, "Maybe I was too hard on my kids." Out of my body I went. I was up and to the right of myself, watching. Their conversation continued. I couldn't hear what was being said, but I could see my niece trying to make eye contact with me. When she did finally make eye contact, I came back. It really was only a matter of seconds. No one knew. She handed me her plate and life went on.

One of the more lengthy and dramatic PTSD events occurred two years ago. My niece and nephew were in from out of town. We were supposed to meet up at my dad and stepmother's condo. I had already decided it was best for me not to stay for dinner. I had made other plans to be with my then-boyfriend. I had been realizing that my "family" was toxic at best. When I arrived the only other people there were Dad and his wife. I started putting appetizers on a plate while I stood in their kitchen. Dad and his wife started fighting. It started with his wife making some snippy remarks about my dad. He started to make snide remarks back. I could feel myself tensing up. They were fighting in the doorway, the only way out of the kitchen. I had my back to them. I kept saying soothing things to myself. I turned around and there was my ninety-two-year-old father with his

and cold. I couldn't stop crying. I never did get any sleep that night. I can tell you I didn't feel safe again around my "family." It didn't matter how much I did with and for them, I was never safe and never secure in knowing any of them had my back in any way. Out of all the PTSD episodes, the uncontrollable shaking, crying, and rerunning it like a movie would be my least favorite. It felt like going into shock. Maybe that's what it truly was.

I don't think I've even had a small PTSD event since May of 2013. That time I was talking to my favorite aunt on the phone, and she started telling me something unflattering that my stepmother had told her about me. Not only was it not nice, but it was untrue. What was it? I don't remember. All I know for sure, I talked a little longer to my aunt and hung up the phone. The next thing I knew, it was two hours later. I popped back into my body and saw I had organized a bunch of closets and drawers. That's how I prefer my PTSD to be, productive. Whatever my aunt told me must've been upsetting. Besides organizing my things, the other good thing that came out of it was I realized I didn't have to have a relationship with my stepmother anymore. Dad was dead, and I owed her nothing. But there will be more about that later. Maybe in its own way, PTSD is productive, maybe with enough therapy…

OCD —obsessive compulsive disorder. That's when people wash their hands a lot, right? Yes, but it's so much more. For me, OCD started with counting. I didn't know it at the time, but I would count how many steps it took me to get from the bus stop to my house when I was in school. I thought it was a fun game I played. But it seemed to me there was a quieter more subtle count going on often. It wasn't until my twenties when I had full-blown anxiety that the OCD became a serious problem. There was incessant counting, washing hands, constant cleaning, and organizing. Certain numbers were problematic, mostly multiples of six. OCD doesn't make sense. While the things that trigger us to do what we do are interesting if you're reading about it as a case study, living it is a much different thing. For me, any thoughts that made me anxious started me counting. When I started to talk to my therapist about it, he said that it had a name, intrusive thinking. For some reason it helped me to

until the wire was picked up. I started to hyperventilate and sweat. I looked left and right. There was no getting around the cars. There was no way to drive across the grass. We were all stuck. I was stuck. And no cell phones back then. I could feel my mounting panic. I was sure I was having a heart attack. I was catastrophizing. I felt sick; I felt I might die right there. I think we sat for almost an hour. Once I got to the store, I couldn't work. I had someone drive me home. I never went back. I couldn't face possibly getting stuck in traffic again. My ability to go anywhere started to dwindle. That's when I went for a mental health intake interview. That's where I met my current therapist. He was the intake doctor. He evaluated me, and then I started seeing a wonderful woman therapist. A lot was going on in my life. I was making a lot of bad choices about things that were causing my full-blown anxiety, which eventually turned into agoraphobia. I did not leave my house by myself for two years. If someone would take me to the grocery store, they had to stay right next to me. Those trips would be short and disorienting. It was hard for me to go get my mail and to go to the laundry room. I had therapy assistants who would help me. I went on Social Security disability so that I could pay my rent. I knew I had to work really hard to get better.

And so the work began. First, I had to learn about agoraphobia. I read <u>Hope and Help for Your Nerves</u> by Claire Weekes. There was a lot of explanation. It would have been interesting reading about it as a case study; living it, not so much. She wrote about different techniques to deal with the anxiety and panic. "Floating through" was one of them. You were supposed to imagine yourself floating away from the anxiety. It worked, but only to a point. Most agoraphobics feel their home is their safe place. But what happens if your panic and anxiety are 24-7? I remember feeling like I had to run away. But to where? I didn't think I had the ability to leave my apartment. I think that's called a double bind. So with me afraid of everything all of the time, history, it just doubled or tripled that feeling. In those two years that I spent in my apartment, I don't remember a lot. I just remember how it felt. How frightening it all was. The first therapist I worked with was great. She suggested trying antianxiety medication. That scared me too. We talked about pros and cons of each drug.

made an appointment to meet with this guy. He had lots of questions about coping skills, symptoms, and limitations. I think we had gotten through about forty-five minutes and I asked him a question. Had anyone told him about the "upside" of agoraphobia? He said, "Upside?" No one said anything like that. I told him the upside was when I did go out and go to, let's say, Target, I could tell him what aisle everything was in, where the bathrooms were, and how far from the front door I was in any aisle I was in. That made my trips out a little easier, for lack of a better word. I could "reason" with my panic somehow. He thought that was really an interesting take on agoraphobia and panic disorders that he had ever heard before. Well, I'm novel, to say the least.

During the worst part of my agoraphobia I saw an Oprah episode with Lucinda Bassett. Lucinda was the founder of the Midwest Center for Stress and Anxiety. She was someone who had suffered through agoraphobia and anxiety and seemed to have come out on the other side. She had put together a packet and cassette tapes that were available for purchase. I listened to her very carefully. She seemed to know "my" disorder intimately. What was amazing to me was she was going to be traveling all over the country giving seminars. She could get on a plane, travel, talk about her disorder, and help others. I just wanted to be able to drive to local destinations without much fear. She was scheduled to be in Minneapolis. My mom offered to take me. Lucinda was going to be at the Minneapolis Convention Center. It was a pretty big place. Overwhelming for me, but I was determined to go. What struck me as funny and logical was when people came in to find their seats, only the end chairs of each row would fill up. All of us needed to know we could get out quickly. In fact, I think the doors were left open as well. Lucinda was and is a brilliant speaker. She told us of her own struggles and triggers. It gave me some hope that someday, even if all the symptoms of panic and anxiety didn't go away, they would be manageable somehow.

Afterward I had the privilege of meeting her. She was warm and welcoming. My mom bought me the tapes. I listened to them in the order I was supposed to. I used the relaxation tape over and over again so I could get some decent sleep. I practiced the techniques,

him some things but held back others. I chose not to tell him about the pregnancy. At one of our later sessions, he suggested my parents should join us so we could talk through my frustration with my family. I agreed. It would be great to have someone on my side and explain how I felt. So the following week, my parents joined me. Before any discussion about my frustration started, the doctor said, "I think she's a terribly troubled child and should be institutionalized." What? Where did that come from? I sat there in utter disbelief. I saw everyone's lips moving but couldn't hear anything. My mind was racing! I was reviewing the things I had told him in the past sessions. Absolutely nothing SHOULD have led to me being put in an institution. I remember thinking how lucky I was I didn't say anything about being pregnant. I would've been sent away for sure. I have no recollection what else happened after that. I never went back to his office. My parents didn't commit me but considered it.

Now I have to flash forward to my early twenties. I met someone through a boyfriend. He told me he used to work at a children's mental institution. He said there were a whole bunch of kids that had been committed by this "lying sack of shit child psychologist." The kids would run down the hallway and snatch the toupee off this doctor's head. They called him "Dr. Frankenstein," which was not too far from his real name. This guy also told me that for each kid he had committed, he got some kind of financial kickback from the state. Guess whose doctor that was? Mine! The one my parents chose for me.

I was told this doctor died a slow painful death from multiple sclerosis. I will just leave that alone...

About a year ago I talked to the daughter of my mom's best friend. We talked about that doctor. She said he got her hooked on drugs, and another friend of hers was molested by this guy. I have no proof of those particular things, but there would be no reason she would make this up at this point. I just feel fortunate that I didn't tell that doctor everything. Can you imagine what would have happened to me?

As I said earlier, I met my current therapist in a mental health intake session. He was the one who referred me to a woman thera-

about burning it. I didn't know. She said she thought it would be a healthy step. I agreed. We walked up the third floor of her building, lit the picture with the lighter, and put it in a container like a ceramic bowl or fire-proof trash bin. As good as it felt, in retrospect I wish I hadn't burned the picture. I heard later my therapist got in trouble for it. I do remember hearing someone say, "I smell smoke" when we were burning the picture. Oh well. *Que sera.*

I reconnected with that therapist I was working with in the days of my agoraphobia. It had been around twenty-five years since we had spoken. I had called and left a message. I was hoping she'd remember who I was. If she didn't, that would be OK. When she called me back, she told me she remembered me. She even went as far as to say there were many people she couldn't remember, but I stood out because she thought I was "precious." I was so excited to hear her voice. We spoke for about a half hour. I even got to take the opportunity to tell her how much she meant to me and what an important role she played in my life. If I'm not mistaken, I started to see her regularly when I was twenty-three until around age twenty-seven. Those were some tough years for me. I had horrible anxiety, acting out, or as I prefer to think of it, trying to live my own life and establishing an identity. What I wanted to know was if she had saved notes from our sessions way back then. We did establish that we were both older now. She couldn't believe I was fifty-five. I told her I would be the only one who got older. She laughed. She said a lot of positive things to me. How she felt about our sessions. What she thought was going on in my life back then. There were so many other things going on, I don't even think I revealed the things I'm writing about now. We agreed that back then I would have preferred to hold my breath than cry. When she said all those nice things to me I was so touched. Before we ended our call, she told me I could call or text her if I needed help with getting the notes from our session from the place she worked at then. She also told me I could call or text to let her know how the book was coming along. The boundary of not getting together for coffee was still firmly in place. But I am forever grateful to her for her compassion and help and got to tell her so. That was very important for me. We ended our call; I sat

When I told him I was going to write this book, he asked me, was I sure I wanted to do this? My answer was an unequivocal yes. Just last week he told me he admired me for taking on this task. We will continue to work together. There is no one I would rather travel this road with.

Anxiety and fear have held me back for years. My new job is to expand my horizons and go on vacation, drive somewhere unfamiliar. I don't have to like it. I don't have to like how I'm feeling while doing it, I just have to apply all the lessons I've learned to be able to go and do whatever. Look my fear in the eye and say, "So what." All I have to do is trust in my own strength. It's gotten me through a lot.

My dad would hit me. Not spank me, but hit me in my head and my face, or grab me and fling me around. When I was in junior high he even broke down the bathroom door right off its hinges and dragged me out "caveman style" by my hair. That was because I told him to shut up. He chased me from the living room while my parents' best friends were sitting there. I got to the bathroom, slammed, and locked the door. When I wouldn't come out, BOOM, the door came down, and out I was dragged and thrown into my room. No one did anything. No one intervened. I was kind of used to my mother not doing anything, but their friends?

I was in constant fear of my dad—afraid of his disapproval, his backhanded compliments, his terrible temper, and his fists.

Another junior high incident, not violence really, just something that didn't make sense. I had bought some wire eyeglass frames out of the "For Sale" section of our junior high paper. They cost me a quarter. I had allowance money and I bought them. I was so excited! We all sat down for dinner, and I took them out to show everyone. I put them on and said, "Aren't these cool?" My dad asked to see them. I took them off and handed them to him. He crushed and twisted them. He started yelling what a waste of money they were. How stupid and irresponsible it was to buy. My throat went dry, everything was blurry, and I was screaming in my head (definitely not out loud) those were mine. I bought them. I was shaken and sat there in disbelief, so angry, but too scared to say or do anything about it. It was never spoken about, ever.

I think I spent the first nine years of my life in my room. I was always grounded, mostly for not finishing my dinner. The thing about that, I never got to choose how much food was put on my plate. My dad was a stickler about "the clean plate club." One time I sat down for dinner and nothing smelled good. I know I was feeling "off." I asked if I could have some eggs instead of whatever was being served. My mom went to the stove with a loud, heavy sigh and started making my eggs. My dad started yelling about it not being a "short-order kitchen." How my mother shouldn't have to cook anything special for me. I was ungrateful, etcetera. Well, I got my scrambled eggs but couldn't finish them. Yes, I was grounded and sent to

ice and was going to call the police. I begged her not to. I told her it would only make things worse. So there I stayed in his dorm, driving myself to high school every day so I could graduate. I think I went home a couple of weeks later to pick up some clothes. My parents wouldn't let anyone come in to help me get my things, so I ran up and down the stairs, bringing things out to the car.

I can tell you that was by far the worst beating I had gotten. I had never felt I was going to die before. But I was afraid, afraid of saying the wrong thing, doing the wrong thing. I had been slapped around quite a bit by my dad. I had gone to school with black eyes and fat lips. Back then no one did anything about it, let alone talked about such things. There weren't many options back then. If I had told anyone, I could have been put into the foster care system but more likely be sent back to my parents' home to suffer the conse-quences of "telling tales." But honestly, I thought everyone had a family like mine. Why would I think any differently? I didn't live in anyone else's house. I knew my parents didn't generally smack me around when I had friends over. I figured that was just how it was. Sad but true. Maybe even back then I had the ability to compart-mentalize. Resiliency? I don't know.

In 1966, my dad almost died from ileitis, now known as Crohn's disease. One night the family was huddled in the northwest corner of the basement because of a terrible storm. My dad suddenly became ill. He and my mom went into the laundry room as my dad was throwing up. I vaguely remember an ambulance being called, but I can't be sure. It may have been something they were talking about. There was a lot of panic. My parents ended up going to the hospital, leaving my sister and me behind. My sister called a friend whose father came and picked us up in the middle of the storm so we wouldn't be alone in our house. We spent the night over there. Either that night or in the following two nights, my dad came near to death. My mom spent her days in the hospital with him. When she finally came home, she said that Dad had turned the corner and was going to be OK. Or as she put it, "He farted." The most beau-tiful sound she'd ever heard. Pretty funny considering she and my dad spent a lot of time shopping for pine-scented matches and air

When I was three or four my dad wanted to cut my toenails and fingernails. I always sat still except for this one time. A piece of skin had overgrown by my baby toe on my right foot. I would play with the skin, especially when I was stressed. How does a three- or four-year-old get stressed? When her parents are fighting and when she knows she could get drawn into the middle of it without even trying. This little piece of skin soothed me. I know it sounds crazy, but it did. So when it came time to cut my toenails, my dad saw the piece of skin. He told me he was going to cut it off. I begged him not to and took off running. He chased me through the house. I finally dove under my parents' king-sized bed. I was crying and begging. He somehow reached me, grabbing me by my ankle, and dragging me out from under the bed. He sat on me, yes sat on me, grabbed my foot, and cut off the piece of dead skin. I remember feeling violated somehow. But of course at three or four, I didn't have the words for it. I just knew it didn't feel right to me that he could do that.

After my mom died, Dad would come to my condo for dinner. He was the only parent I had left, and I wanted to try to have a decent relationship with him. Every time he came over, he was rude. I realize now that I was "SHOULDING." I thought I SHOULD have him over, I thought I SHOULD try to have a normal relationship with him. I now realize it takes two to forge a relationship. He would talk about the most inappropriate things. Picking up women, should he buy condoms, etcetera. Sex was always a topic he liked to talk about. It was so lascivious. But he was always like that. He didn't seem to have any common sense as to what was appropriate to talk to his daughter about. So eventually, the dinners stopped. I couldn't listen to the sex stuff or to his opinion of me. Even though I had a career of my own, a company of my own, he thought I should be selling cars. We all know how people feel about car salesmen. They're considered lower than ambulance-chasing attorneys. Why would this be something he would want me to do? I didn't find it flattering at all. But then he had a lot of opinions about me that were unflattering.

My dad remarried a year and a half after my mom died. That is a whole chapter on its own. His remarriage gave us an extended step-family. One of the stepgrandkids had a Bar Mitzvah. I was invited

with immediate family or stepfamily. It seemed that the worst things happened in the Rosh Hashanah/Yom Kippur timeframe.

As I got into my forties, my excuse for continuing to go to these painful, dysfunctional holiday or family gatherings was that my dad was in his eighties and how much time would be left? Or in other words, how much time could possibly be left? So I "SHOULD" myself into going. I would help serve food and help clear the dishes. I figured that it was harder to hit a moving target when it came to all the negativity. It didn't always work. I would go to these things and try to stay under the radar.

Ah, my fortieth birthday! I had waited my entire life to turn forty. Somehow I had the impression that once I turned forty everything would be a breeze. For me, forty represented an inauguration of wisdom, health, peace, and security. Ha! I was about to learn there really is no "magic" age.

I wanted to throw a fun, unique fortieth birthday party for myself—something that my friends would love as much as I would. There was only one answer. Casey Jones. For the non-Minnesotans who are reading this, Casey Jones was a local TV personality. He dressed like a train conductor and would "arrive on track 11." When I was growing up, he had a noontime show called "Lunch with Casey." He and his sidekick, Roundhouse Rodney, would perform skits and songs, have lunch, introduce cartoons, and just generally have fun. For me, his show was the only time there was no fighting, screaming, or hitting. I loved him for that.

About a month before my birthday, I was at my dad's, and he and his wife asked me what I wanted for my fortieth birthday. What kind of party? So I told them. I want to have Casey Jones at my party. It didn't take more than a minute. My dad started yelling at me. "That's the dumbest thing I've ever heard." Let the berating begin. I told him I wasn't asking him to pay for it, but that was what I was going to do. I don't know why I was so stunned by his venomous reaction. I could feel myself start to shake and feel sick. I had to leave…fast! I think he was still going on and on when I put on my coat, picked up my purse, and left. I can honestly tell you I don't remember the drive home. The next thing I remember is sitting

get to have a private moment with Casey to let him know what he meant to me. That he was a peaceful part of my life. He hugged me and then he had to leave.

Something else came from that party. I was going to pay Casey his guest appearance fee, but my dad had already done it. Hmmmm, odd. I asked him about it the next day. He told me he realized that the people he saw at my party were people he had seen with me most of my life. This is a man that told me from when I was eight or nine that I couldn't get along with anybody. I always thought that was a strange thing to say since my friends have been with me for years. So I guess that was some kind of admission that he had been wrong about something. He also thought it was a great party. He was surprised during the sing-along portion. We all knew the words to all of Casey's songs. It was a great day all around. Did that mean my dad was coming around? Nah. But it was nice for that day.

At eighty-one, Dad had quadruple bypass surgery. Pretty stressful for all of us. But he came through with flying colors. One of his proudest moments was when the doctor told him that he had a hard time getting the vein out of my dad's leg because his legs were so muscular. My dad, the jock. Fewer things were more important to him than his physical appearance and ability to work out. It would be months after his bypass that he would be able to work out again. But he did it. As he got later into his eighties, there were some health scares: pneumonia, spinal stenosis. As he got into his nineties, there was what appeared to be bladder cancer. He was scheduled for surgery to have what they thought was a tumor removed. We all gathered at the hospital and waited for him to be prepped for surgery. They said it would probably be an hour. So my sister, stepmother, and I went to the cafeteria to get something to eat. As we sat down to patiently wait, the pager we were carrying started blinking with a "come back to the waiting room" message. It had only been twenty minutes, maybe a half hour. We all looked at each other. Nothing much was said. We gathered our stuff and went back to the waiting room and did just that, waited. About a half hour later the doctor came out and said it was a blood clot. As soon as he touched it, it dissipated. I know we were all expecting the doctor to tell us Dad

groceries online and that they would deliver it to them. He would calm down and go back to sleep. I told the nurses and caregivers to say that to him.

The day before he died, I went to visit him and knew it wouldn't be much longer. I took him by his hands and asked him to look at me. He opened his eyes and looked right into mine. I said, "I forgive you for being an awful father." He squeezed my hands and closed his eyes. I stayed a little while longer and then I went home.

The following morning around eight thirty I went over to see him. He was really weak. His eyes were closed. I don't even think he knew I was there. I sat on the bed and didn't say much. I kissed him on his forehead and left. At one o'clock I got a call from my sister saying Dad had died. I told her I would be right there. I called my best friend and asked her to meet me there. I needed her by my side. Little did I know how much. You would think this would be the end of the story, but it's not. The saga continues in the stepfamily chapter.

him grab me, take me to the shallow end, and start spanking me. She saw, I know she did! I screamed for her, and she turned around and walked out. I realized in that instant I was on my own. On more than one occasion, he would have me floating on my back in the middle of the pool. If I became anxious or what he deemed difficult, he would push my head up and out of the water so that I would go under. I would flail around to try to save myself, and he would make sure I would go under again. Of course then I would start to cry and you know what happened next...I don't remember much else about it. I don't know if I quit swimming or the amount of lessons were over. I can tell you to this day I am not fond of swimming. I can swim, but I am much better standing in a pool or treading water without getting my head wet.

Next I tried skating. I was around seven. I liked the teacher. I liked that she was patient and kind. I recall wearing winter coats with furry cuffs and collars with warm gloves. It was very "Currier and Ives." I skated for years. I liked it. I had good balance. I wasn't really interested in becoming a professional skater. I just wanted to be able to skate well and not get hurt. Well, we all know that's good in theory. I was skating one afternoon, fell, and somebody skated over my finger opening up a gash to the bone. All that blood...ugh! I had to be taken to the doctor and have stitches. Skating was not the same after that. I became scared. Remember, I was afraid of everything all of the time.

For as long as I could remember, my mom worked. She had a home office where she wrote a cake-decorating magazine. There was a main office where she delivered her work. I would go with her quite often. The ladies there were so nice. They were all so friendly to me. One lady always had candy in a bowl on her desk. Every time I was there, she would smile at me and offer me some. I would wander around and say hi to everyone. I could even go into the warehouse and jump into a pile of packing worms, just like leaves on a fall day. I was happy when I was there.

Mom had gone out to dinner at a downtown restaurant. Several days later she didn't feel well. She thought she had food poisoning. She went to the doctor and was diagnosed with non-Hodgkin's lym-

thing I didn't want to have this conversation. She said I needed to tell her, "Because in your grief, your sister will roll all over you." I was shocked at how cold that statement was regarding her own daughter. She said it so matter-of-factly. It's not that I necessarily disagreed, but it was so shocking. And I realized at that moment I thought I had a secret to keep. My sister didn't need to know what my mom said or how she felt about her. I felt sick. The only people I told were my closest friends. I told them how awful it was and how my sister SHOULD never be told. It has pained me for over twenty-two years. Now that moment in time doesn't have to be my responsibility anymore. In fact, it never was. It was just another "SHOULDING" of my own doing.

I know we all breathed a sigh of relief when Mom was cancer-free for a couple of years. In fact, we had a party to celebrate. I had invited a bunch of people to my mom and dad's to celebrate my mom's birthday. I had spent months crocheting her an afghan that matched the bright-colored furniture in their basement. Every waking moment, every break at work, I crocheted. I finished it the day before the party. I wrapped it in a big box with a bow. The day of the party I brought the box over and put it downstairs where the guests would be putting their gifts. It was a lovely party. Mom and Dad were happy to have their friends around. We ate, talked, drank and then came time to open the gifts. My mom opened each gift with care. She would read the card and thank each person profusely. Then it came time to open my gift. I was so excited to see the look on her face! She opened it, picked up the corner of the afghan, read my card and looked at me, and said thank you, sort of in a monotone. Anticlimactic would be an understatement. I thought she'd be so excited. I guess I was wrong. Maybe she didn't like it at all. I couldn't tell. After more socializing, people started to leave. After the last guest was gone my mom came up to me to tell me she loved my gift and didn't think she should show any more excitement than the other gifts because she didn't want to make her guests feel bad. What? I didn't get it, but that's the way she thought she should play it. She did use that afghan all the time. At least that's something.

When I was little, my mom liked to brush my hair. She especially liked to put my hair in really tight pigtails. She would pull them so tight! If I would complain she was hurting me, she would hit me in the head with the brush, or she would clap me on my ears really hard. I remember coming back from sleep away summer camp and telling her how good it felt to do my own hair and feel independent. I didn't realize then it was more about not getting hit in the head anymore.

In elementary school I started taking dance lessons: jazz, tap, ballet, and acrobatics. I loved it! I loved learning. I loved the movement. It made me happy. In junior high I started dancing with the Minnesota Dance Theater and School. Two friends and I would take the bus to Dinkytown, walk from the bus stop down the block to the dry cleaners. We would walk up the stairs behind the dry cleaners, and there was the studio. It was a very exciting place to be. It was completely different from other places I had taken lessons. It was more prestigious because some of the students had a chance to audition for the Minnesota Dance Theater's production of Loyce Houlton's *The Nutcracker Suite*. I danced at the school for a couple of years and then decided to audition for *The Nutcracker*. There were so many young girls and boys there to try out to be a soldier or a mouse. They knew they were only going to pick seven of us out of the hundred that were there. I was nervous and so excited! Who knew? It could have been the beginning of a career. So there were several rounds of auditions. Then we all sat there waiting to hear if we had been chosen. My mom had driven me there and was sitting up in the balcony with the other parents. They started calling out names. I was one of them! I was going to be a mouse. How exciting! I would work hard and learn so much. I would work in the dance theater company and earn my way to other auditions and parts. It seemed the sky was the limit. They asked the parents of those of us who were chosen to join them downstairs. We all sat together and were told what was expected. There would be four rehearsals a week. The parents would give out programs. There were other things, but I really don't remember what they were. Oh, how exciting. The theater! What a beginning.

After the Minnesota Dance Theater, I didn't know if I wanted to dance anymore. It was such a blow not to be dancing in *The Nutcracker Suite*. Even now when I see advertising for Lisa Houlton's production of *The Nutcracker*, I can barely breathe. I will never know if I would have gone on to choose dance as a career or get tired of it on my own. (For my fifty-fifth birthday present my best friend bought tickets for the Minnesota Dance Theater's fifty-year anniversary production of *The Nutcracker Suite*. I was prepared for whatever feelings would come my way. I can honestly say, it was magical and very healing for me).

I think it was my mother that found the Andahazy School of Ballet. It was close to our house and much more "convenient." My parents told me if I really loved dancing, I could take classes there. So I thought I'd try it. I was balancing school, skiing, basketball, and Vocaleers (choir and volleyball) at the same time. But I did want to dance. Andahazy Ballet was worlds away from the Minnesota Dance Theater. Andahazy was a strict Russian ballet school and dance Company, while the Minnesota Dance Theater and School was much more lighthearted and thrived on the creativity of their staff and students. Mr. Andahazy was tough. He didn't smile much. He was aggressive, yelled, and belittled the students. Suffice it to say if I wanted to be treated like that, I could just stay home. But I wanted to give it a try. I think I lasted one month. I was at the barre doing a plié and my knee locked. The same knee I had injured the previous year skiing. Mr. Andahazy came up to me and instructed me to straighten my legs and stand up straight. I told him I couldn't, my knee was locked. I told him I had injured it skiing. He told me I had to choose between dancing or skiing. I couldn't do both. He walked around with a stick that he would hit the ground to keep time to the music. When I told him I liked both skiing and dancing, he hauled off and hit my leg with that pointy stick. That was my last day at Andahazy. I had danced for nine years, and no instructor had ever hurt me until that day. I gave up dance. I didn't know what else to do or where else to go where I would feel safe. So again, I will never know if I could've had a career in dance. Disco doesn't count.

I sang in my junior high choir. We not only had a choir, but the choir also competed in volleyball. I loved singing. I had a high tenor to second soprano range. That allowed me to sing all kinds of harmonies. We did Christmas concerts around the Twin Cities and one big school concert every year. Our choir teacher made it fun. We sang in different languages in two of the three concerts I was in. It was a lot of work and a lot of fun. I tried out for the school talent show. A friend of mine (one of "my family of choice") played piano while we sang. We didn't make it into the show, but that was all right. I was very nervous. Believe it or not, with all of my dance, guitar, and singing experience, I had terrible stage fright.

Our school concert was coming up and the theme was "Around the World in Just One Night," which was not to be mistaken for "Around the World a Second Time" the following year. The choir director approached me and asked me if I wanted to play a stewardess to give the flight instructions before we took off on our around the world tour. I said absolutely. I called Northwest Airlines and spoke to someone about the exact "seat and tray tables in their upright and locked position" speech. The woman I spoke to gave me her name, and I asked her if she wanted to come see the show. She said she did. I left her a ticket; she didn't show up. But that's OK. I went and bought the stewardess-like outfit complete with beret and white go-go boots. When the show started I entered from the back of the auditorium and walked all the way up the center aisle to the stage. I grabbed a microphone and welcomed everyone aboard. I gave the whole spiel about emergencies, etcetera, and then the show would start. I think the concert was about one and a half hours. We did the show twice in two days. It was amazing. I learned a lot of different languages and learned about other cultures. It was fun. I was happy.

Since this chapter is about my mom, I have to flash forward from my junior high years of 1972 to 1974, to my twenties, somewhere around1982 to 1983. I don't know how this particular conversation got started. When I was living on my own in my first apartment, I was on the phone with my mom. I don't even remember what we were talking about, but she brought up the junior high concert. Odd, but OK…Out of the blue she says, "When you didn't make the tal-

I looked at prices first. It was probably a good thing I became allergic to seafood when I was twenty-three and stopped eating red meat when I was thirty.

There was a lot of shaming of me from my mother. She used guilt and manipulation. I just thought that was par for the course in being Jewish. Her using guilt was not at all lighthearted. It was to try and bend me to her will. I was working full-time at The Limited. On my day off, my boss called and said she needed me to do something for her. I asked my mom if I could borrow her car (because I didn't have a car of my own). She said OK. I drove out to the store, ran the errand my boss needed me to run, stopped at a shoe store, and then drove home. When I got there, my mom was in the front yard in a two-tone blue Hawaiian print bikini standing next to the waterfall sprinkler. She was splashing herself with water. I stopped the car in the driveway, got out, and she said, "I was invited to our country club, but I couldn't go because you had the car. So this is my pool, *this* is my pool." I was only gone a couple of hours if that. I told her she had plenty of time to get to the club. Honestly, it was two o'clock in the afternoon. There were no cell phones back then, but she could have called the store to let me know she needed me to come home right away. So there she stood, in her bikini next to the sprinkler repeating, "This is my pool."

In my mid-twenties my mom asked me to come over to her house. She wanted to know how I did my makeup. She said she wanted her eyes to look "dirty" like mine. I figured she actually meant smoky. I took her into the bathroom and applied my eye shadow. I have to tell you, this is not even 20-20 hindsight. It gave me a really creepy and uneasy feeling. I was applying the color. She had heavier skin on her eyelids (like I do now at age fifty-five). The shadow was hard to apply as was the notion that she wanted her look to be like mine. My mom was always a fashion-plate. But I couldn't shake this feeling. Then it occurred to me, she was in competition for my youth. She had borrowed clothes from me to wear to parties, even though she had closets full of clothes. Just the thought of her being in competition for my youth made me queasy. And overthinking it, as I have been known to do, did that mean I was in competition

family for that matter, needed. Just another pattern I didn't become aware of until much later.

My boyfriend proposed in 1987. What a joyous thing to plan a wedding, right? Maybe other people…mine, not so much. First we told our families. Then we were off and running planning the wedding. Besides the date, my fiancé left pretty much everything up to me. Flowers, music, bridesmaids, food, etcetera. I ended up doing a lot of this with my mother. I wanted a smaller wedding because my fiancé had been married and divorced. I thought that would be the tasteful thing to do. What I SHOULD do? I had a good idea what I wanted invitations to look like, something simple with an abstract flower on it. So off my mother and I went to look at invitations. There they were, after looking through several sample books, the perfect invitation. Off-white with a light coral colored abstract flower on the front. Beautiful and reasonably priced. I loved them. I took the sample out, I knew this was it! I told my mom we could stop looking, that I found exactly what I was looking for. She took one look at it and said, "No, that's not what you're going to use for an invitation." She didn't have any valid reason, just no. So she proceeded to pick out and order what she wanted. I just didn't want to fight. It was a run of the mill off-white invitation with gold embossed lettering. I figured the message would be the same, "come to our wedding." Besides, I didn't have the energy for what I thought would turn into a big battle.

Flowers were a little easier. She seemed to like my choices. I just wanted them to be low-key and tasteful. The dresses, well that was interesting. I gave my mom, sister, and my maid of honor a color pallet. Any shade of rose. I asked them all to be tasteful and more importantly be something they could wear again. I didn't want bridesmaid looking dresses. Just cocktail length, anything in the rose family. Sounds easy, right? Everyone gets to buy what fits their taste. I couldn't have made it easier. The only one to handle the task with no drama was my maid of honor. She had someone make her a dress in a rose color. Easy-peasy. My sister and mother, on the other hand, were talking about embellishments and poofs. So I ended up having to go shopping with both of them. My sister bought a beautiful medium

left the dress with her and walked out. When I went back a couple weeks later, the dress was back to the way it SHOULD'VE been and SHOULD'VE stayed!

Flash-forward to just a couple years ago, I was telling one of my close girlfriends about the dress incident. This particular girlfriend has clothes tailored all of the time. She said she had never heard of any tailor taking on that kind of extra work without being told to do so. I know I didn't tell her to do it. Should we speculate who called her friend that owned the bridal shop? I can. I have no proof my mother did this because the woman that owned the shop died years ago, and the shop closed even before she died. I'm left to wonder. But my three closest friends agree this sounded like something my mom would have done. How it never crossed my mind at the time, I don't know. Maybe it SHOULD have.

We had our wedding reception at a country club. Before the dress incident, my mom and I went out to the country club to talk to the caterer. He was such a nice guy and did his job well. He presented us with many options: per-plate dinners, buffet style, appetizers. I told him what I thought would be good to serve from the kitchen, as opposed to a buffet. My mom decided it was going to be a buffet. She wouldn't let me get a word in edgewise. It was actually more like her wedding, her choices. It was all so frustrating. I stopped talking. I totally shut down. She signed all the agreements with the caterer, and we drove home. I talked to my fiancé about how she had belittled and humiliated me by talking down to me regarding anything I wanted for the reception. Remember, my fiancé didn't want to be involved. The only thing he wanted was an open bar and a small boutonniere for his suit jacket. Otherwise everything else was up to me. I asked him how he felt about a very small wedding and reception. He was fine with it.

The next day I called the caterer and canceled everything. My fiancé and I started talking about a much smaller venue and a party later on. I really had had enough…I thought. I talked to my mom the next day and told her I had canceled everything, and my fiancé and I were going to do this on our own without so much drama. If I recall, she hung up on me. A few hours later, my father showed up at

to make money. What I wasn't happy with was before the cocktail hour started, my mother was being exceptionally rude to him. I went over and apologized to him. I told him she had been difficult at best during this whole wedding process. I'm so glad he didn't blame me, or worse yet leave and take his band with him.

Many years later, after I had gotten married, I was over at her house, and we were standing in her driveway. She started talking to me about kids. I think I had been married a little over a year. She started trying to "sell" me on the idea of having a child. "Sell" is a little light. Guilt me into having a baby is more accurate. Mind you, my sister had two kids, so she already had grandchildren. She said to me, a child from me would be the most special child ever. No child would ever be loved more. I thought that was odd because she already had grandchildren that she loved a lot. It struck me as the "most wanted baby in America" thing she had told me about myself. It did feel she was turning up the pressure a bit. I was twenty-eight at the time. After growing up in the abusive atmosphere, not just the guilt, the shaming, the belittling, I'm talking about the physical abuse, I had decided not to have children. I wasn't 100 percent sure I could break the cycle of violence. I wouldn't want to put a child through what I went through. I had done a lot of reading and research. There was nothing that would guarantee I would be able to stop myself from perpetuating violence. It scared me. But again, I was afraid of everything, all of the time. Are we sensing a theme? What I didn't realize was that I was so aware of my background, it would have prevented me from being that way. I'll get into that in another chapter.

Many years later, Mom got sick again. This time it wasn't non-Hodgkin's lymphoma, it was myelodysplastic syndrome (most recently brought to light by Robin Roberts on *Good Morning America*). From what I understood the doctors told us it had to do with the chemo that Mom had had. What happened was the myelodysplasia turned into acute leukemia after some time. I'm a little hazy on how long that took. My parents vacationed every year in Palm Springs, California. Their last trip Mom had to be air-ambulanced back here. She had a bunch of tests that concluded she had acute leukemia, and the family was told she only had three weeks to live. She

I was throwing up?" She smiled. "And whose mother would go find buckets of water to clean up the parking lot when I threw up on the doctor's office parking lot?" She tried to laugh. She said, "But you are my baby." And I said, "Why don't you let me do this, and you be my baby now." Nothing else was said. That was my last conversation with her. She died two days later. I got a call from my dad March 6, and he said, "She's gone." He had gone to take a shower and when he went to check on her she had passed.

When I got there, she was still warm. My aunt (my mom's sister) saw the look in my eyes and said to me, "Let's say the Shema." The Shema is a Jewish prayer, which is the centerpiece of all Jewish prayers. It was a wonderful thing for her to do. I needed some direction. It was perfect. I will always be grateful to her for that.

Now that I have written these things down and reread them, I realize there's a pattern with my mother. Whatever made me happy, be it dance, guitar, planning a wedding, she made sure to try and ruin it for me or at least take credit for what I had accomplished on my own. I will never know why she was that way. But because of the horrible relationship I had with my father, I figured I SHOULD love her twice as much. The truth is, neither of them could be trusted to keep me safe.

That was the big epiphany at age fifty-one. Not only was my mother complicit in my abuse, she generally set it up by getting my dad enraged. I didn't stand a chance...

must be what's wrong with me according to her. She thinks it's funny. Ha-ha…*Not!*

As I got older, I tried being helpful. If she was sick, I would bring her groceries. One particular time I picked up a couple of bags of groceries for her. I called her from her apartment lobby and asked her to meet me at the elevator. At the time I was terrified of elevators. So I put the groceries in the elevator and ran up the stairs. I stepped out of the stairwell and the elevator was just opening. My sister was in the hallway, and all she could say was, "This isn't very convenient, you know." Not thank you. But I persevered. I would babysit her kids. If she went out of town I would stay at her house to take care of my niece and nephew. No real heartfelt thank-yous were given, just an expectation of me being able to help her. That was fine if we were going to bond like sisters SHOULD. There's that word again. I don't know why I wasn't catching a clue that a sisterly relationship was probably never going to happen.

When I was fifteen, I contracted mono. Every year my parents went to Palm Springs for a month or more for vacation. That year I was so sick, but my parents decided to go anyway leaving me with my sister and her first husband to take care of me. They moved into my parents' house. When they pulled up into the driveway, they got out of their car and came inside. The first thing my sister said was, "Go out and get our bags." What? Not wanting to cause myself any problems I went out and dragged in their luggage. Then she told me to fix dinner. Now really, who would want someone with mono cooking for them? After dinner I was sitting on the floor wrapping presents, and my sister told me to clean up what I was doing. I told her I was almost done. She started yelling, walked over, and started hitting me in the face and head. I grabbed her hand and dug my fingernails into the back of her hand until she was bleeding. I just wanted her to stop hitting me. She knew better! She didn't like it when Dad hit her. None of it made any sense to me. But what happened next was mind-blowing. Her husband ran over, hit me, and said, "Look what you've done to your sister!" These were the people who were supposed to take care of me. These were the people I was supposed to rely on? How was I going to get well? What was I sup-

washed her hair and got the mud off of her. I dried her off, wrapped her in a towel, and sat her in the rocking chair. Unfortunately, she rocked herself out of the chair and into a crumpled heap on the floor. While this was happening, my sister was still going on and on about her boyfriend. I finally told her to leave the room and go to sleep. I just couldn't believe what her priorities seemed to be. A little askew I would say. I got a dry, clean T-shirt from my sister and planned to stay awhile. I really wanted to keep my niece sitting up and awake. After an hour or so I finally put her to bed. The only all-night programming back then was roller derby. So I sat up all night watching roller derby and every twenty minutes made sure my niece was breathing. About 7:00 a.m. I decided to go home with my souvenir "Welcome to Jamaica" T-shirt. I never gave it back. You know the saying "My sister called, my niece was drunk and thrown from a moving car, and all I got was this lousy T-shirt…"

My Family—The Fowl Experience

Over the years my sister and I have gotten together for family dinners. I would call them family functions but that would be a misnomer. For years I've cooked and transported the turkey for Thanksgiving. This particular year, Thanksgiving was at my sister and her fiancé's house. I was told to be there at six thirty. So I timed the roasting and resting of the turkey for that time. I spent my day off trying to relax. At two thirty I got a call from my sister saying she wanted a hot turkey served. I told her you don't serve hot turkey because it won't slice right. You need it to rest a bit and cool off. She started yelling she wanted hot turkey. Again, the theme with my sister. Not wanting to cause any problems, I would bring a hot turkey. Transporting a twenty-five-pound hot turkey, juices sloshing, was going to be a trick. So at five thirty I put the turkey back in the oven. At six o'clock my sister called and said, "Where are you?" I reminded her she had called me at home. She wanted to know why I wasn't there. I reminded her she told me six thirty. She started screaming at me about how wrong I was. I could hear people in the background. Clearly her guests were already there. She said she wanted me there now! I again reminded

on, but the girlfriend, stepson, and I could barely look at each other all night. That wasn't stressful, not at all.

The most ridiculous and painful things happened because of family gatherings. I can recall so many hurtful, embarrassing things that happened starting from when I was a child up until just recently.

Keeping with the sister theme, in 2011 my sister invited the family to her house for dinner. My niece, her husband, and their kids were here from out of town. I was really looking forward to seeing how much the kids had grown and also catching up with what my niece had been up to. I was on my way over to pick up my dad and his wife when my cell phone rang. It was my sister. She said, "I don't think I cooked anything you can eat." Now to tell you the truth, this didn't surprise me. But really who does that? As usual this made it appear that something else was my fault. Now it was somehow picky eating. The first thing I said was, "What do you want me to do? Put a chicken in my purse?" She became miffed by my attitude. Before she could say anything else I asked, "Is there salad?" She said there was. I replied, "Then there's something I can eat."

When we arrived the kids were sitting at the table eating spaghetti noodles with butter and bread. In the sink there was a colander full of noodles. As we settled into eat, I asked if I could have some noodles. My sister yelled to my niece, "Could Roberta have some noodles or will the kids want seconds?" My niece said of course I could, and the kids wouldn't want any more. So I put some noodles on my plate and put the plate in the microwave. Unfortunately she had a microwave that you need to be a rocket scientist to work. I stood there reading the different buttons. The next thing I knew I was shoulder blocked out of the way by my sister and in her most condescending and bitter tone said, "Oh just let me do it." Begging the question, why do I go to these things? After that tension-filled meal, I was glad to go home. Again, why do I go in the first place? Because, for some reason I think I SHOULD. I SHOULD spend time with my elderly father. I SHOULD spend time with my family, however dysfunctional it may be. After much contemplation, I determined I was just afraid. Afraid of rocking the boat, afraid of people being mad, afraid of emotional maybe even physical abuse.

disorder and how anxious she was feeling through this process. Ah, a moment of support! She asked my then-husband not to go on his business trip because things were near the end with my mom. After they bickered back and forth, he relented and stayed in town. So pretty much there they are, the moments of support. Even when my dad died, she wasn't very helpful to me. No sisterly connection, some discussion, no connection and lots of judgment.

In 1988, my then husband and I were giving a Chanukah party at our house. Friends and family were invited. I got a call from my sister telling me she wanted to bring four of her friends with her. I told her we didn't really have the seating space. She told me she wouldn't come unless she could bring these people. I knew if she didn't come it would upset our parents, and I'd never hear the end of it. So we squeezed everyone in.

In 2000, my sister decided to have Thanksgiving at her house. I was long divorced by then. I asked if I could bring my best friend and her husband with me. They were in town for just a few days. She said no. I asked her one more time. She again said no. So my friend and I had our own peaceful Thanksgiving. The best part of not being there was hearing from my stepmother the next day. Evidently my brother-in-law tried a new recipe he found online that said you can cook a fifteen- to twenty-pound turkey in a convection oven in an hour. Well, it didn't work out so well. The turkey wasn't served until after 8:00 p.m. So glad I got to miss out on the drama of that "family gathering."

Our mom died March 6, 1994. Passover was three or four weeks after that. This would be our first Passover without Mom. The week before she died, I was sitting with her, and she asked me if I knew how to make "the soup." I knew she was referring to the big stockpot full of chicken soup with matzo balls for Passover. She told me the recipe and said she had a secret ingredient but I SHOULDN'T tell anyone—and by the way, I never have. So of course it was up to me to make the soup for Passover. Even though I was doing the majority of the cooking, Passover was going to be at Dad's house. As I was making the soup in that same stockpot my mom had used, I was standing in my own kitchen cooking, crying and definitely feeling

body. I'm sure it was a PTSD reaction. I heard myself say, "Once Dad is gone, you're going to find a reason not to have anything to do with me." And that is exactly what has happened. We haven't spoken since October 2013, and I don't expect we will. Our last conversation was regarding MNSure, Minnesota's answer to the Affordable Health Care Act. She wanted to help me sign up. Obviously she didn't think I could do it on my own. She wanted to come over and help me. I told her I would take care of it on my own. I got off the phone and sat there thinking that her opinion of me wasn't really any different than my father's or mother's. I waited a day and decided to send her an e-mail explaining her how I felt. Our last exchanges were e-mails as follows:

> I spent some time thinking about what to say to you. When you called yesterday to offer me your "help" with signing up for MNSure, I didn't know what to say. So I didn't say much of anything. But now that I've had a chance to think about it, I find your suggestion to come over and "help" intrusive, insulting and just plain condescending. What would make you think I would need your help, or that I would want to share any of my personal information with you? You haven't exactly been "helpful" to me in the past. If you are so fascinated by MNSure, go online and read about it. FYI: The site was still down this morning. It's up and running now. I've even taken care of everything all by myself!!
>
> Roberta

∽o∾

> *I'm on a break at work so this will be quick. As usual you misconstrued what I was saying/asking and of course your way is always and only the right way. If I wanted to do as you said here. I would have called*

that. She sent me a card for my birthday. At that time the one-year anniversary of my dad's death was looming. I wasn't sure how I felt about it. As I said in the opening of the book, the irony didn't escape me that I started to write a year to the day after his death. My dad's Yahrzeit was the weekend of January 10 to 12, 2014. That would be one Friday night service and two short fifteen-minute services on Saturday and Sunday. On January 9, I received an e-mail from my sister, subject line: "Letting you know." "Just wanted you to know we are bringing [stepmother] to the six o'clock Saturday evening service at Temple." That's it. That's all it said. I couldn't decide if it was a warning, a shot across the bow, if you will, or was it an, "if you'd like to see us that's when we'll be there." My impression, it was a warning. It certainly was no invitation. I had been struggling with whether I wanted to attend the service and honor my father at all. As it happened, I did not go to any of the services. I didn't go to my mother's a month later either. That was the first time in twenty-one years. Those decisions I made in 2014 don't have to be permanent, I just have to honor my own feelings first.

So you would think that this chapter about my sister would be done. How could there be more? We aren't speaking. Well, in my family even that doesn't stop strange things from happening, but that's another story that's in another chapter. Because we are not speaking, that means I'm hearing nothing about my niece and her family or my nephew. I had a strong feeling I should call my niece. I do have to add at this point my niece and nephew are not great at getting back to people. It's nothing personal, just the way it is. I called my niece on a Wednesday and left a message saying I just wanted to say hi and see how everything was and hoped everything was OK. I hadn't heard back by Friday, so I texted her and said, "Left you a message on Wednesday, hope everything is OK." I got a text back within a few minutes that said, "Hi! Just starting to be able to talk and focus. Thank you for the message! I'm good, healing. They got all the cancer, so I'm very happy." What? I texted back "Cancer…I know nothing. I'm calling, answer your phone." She texted back, "Sure."

So I called, and we talked. I said, "What cancer?" She said, "You know I had thyroid cancer." A couple of years ago, yeah. "Well they

CHAPTER 6

Me

So I thought I would write about my expectations of having a "family." I don't know where my expectations came from, they were just there. Maybe better put what I thought a family SHOULD be. For as long as I can remember, I thought a family was who you lived with, who loved you unconditionally and supported your dreams, ambitions, and aspirations. Is this a Pollyanna view? I didn't think so. I always operated with the notion that my family would be those people, even if it was shown to me to be otherwise. I don't think my belief in unconditional love and acceptance wavered. Whatever physical or emotional abuse happened, I still believed that "my family" would be there for me no matter what. It has become clear to me after writing for so many months about living and dealing with my so-called family, that that was never the case.

Recently I was talking to my therapist and asking him how I couldn't see this sooner. As I said, I started understanding what happened throughout my life with "my family" when I was fifty-one. And even then it was just the tip of the iceberg. He told me I had to believe what I was thinking, that they were there for me because I had no choice. And then my therapist said something that made my heart sink and made me sick to my stomach. A bombshell "Aha moment." He said, "Even abused dogs look to their abusers to feed

with someone. Sonny and Cher's "I've Got You Babe." I shook while I sang, but I was doing it. Now you can't pry that microphone out of my cold dead hand. I've been singing at karaoke places for fifteen years. I'm still nervous every time I get up to walk to the stage, but I still do it. I can tell you I don't think I sing full out, and I'm never satisfied with how I sound. I always find fault. No one else does, just me.

Back to singing lessons. I got a booklet regarding community education, and there was a voice-lesson class listed. I decided now was the time. I was going to explore my voice, learn the ins and outs, what my voice would and would not support. After a couple of weeks, I signed up for class. The instructor was wonderful. She taught us a lot about breath control, tone quality, and adjustments. She taught me about what I called my falsetto. It's actually called a "whistle register." So much to learn. The first week the students and instructor didn't do much singing. We did do voice warm-up exercises and sang scales. Our homework assignment was to pick a song to sing in class that we could work on for the next few weeks. So many songs, so many choices. My first thought was to sing something I always sing when I'm at karaoke. Nope, not going to do that. Pick something meaningful and emotional. Nope, I don't need to break down crying in class. Pick something that runs my entire range. Nope. Pick something unexpected that I would never sing at karaoke. Something that I love. Show tunes! *Guys and Dolls.* My favorite, especially when I'm listening to the original Broadway soundtrack. "If I Were a Bell" was my choice. It was fun, animated, and in my "whistle register" where I love to sing. I practiced all week and was sure it was the right choice…until an hour and a half before class. Nerves got the best of me. But I went with it anyway. I got to class and was a little shaky. The time arrived for me to sing. The two guys in my class chose me to go first. I think in show business it's called "flop sweat." I sang, I hit all the notes, my breath control was good…surprisingly. My hands were sweating, and it was a very long three minutes. I got done, took a deep breath, and waited for the criticism. There wasn't any. The instructor had me play with the tone in my voice when I sang it for the second time. I knew I had to learn to

and lazy. I wish I could have filtered out all of the negativity and untruth. It took me years of therapy and practice, practice, practice to stop playing those old tapes. Even now, knowing better, a snippet of an old tape will play. I have to stop and ask myself where that came from and why. It usually has to do with some anxiety, however small, I'm feeling. But I really do know the truth. I am a good person. I am smart. I have long-term great friendships that mean the world to me. Those people see me for who I truly am. Those are the things that matter most to me.

I don't want to upset myself, but I write anyway. How does that song go? "Feelings, nothing more than feelings…" The impact of seeing the book come to fruition is deep. The writing is daunting. I know that I'm trying to save the "lighter stuff" to write down later. Maybe that will make it all worth it. I've told many people that writing the book will be good for me. Best-case scenario, number one: it will help someone going through the things I went through. Best-case scenario, number two: I'll publish this book, it will be well-received, and I'll make money off my crazy-ass family. In my fertile fantasy life, Oprah will call, telling me she's picked my book for her book club. I'll be able to meet her and maybe Tyler Perry too. Even Iyanla Vanzant will want to talk to me about my resiliency. Like I said, fertile fantasy life.

also admitted she liked to be involved in getting me upset so they could see my parents get angry and yell at them. She also said they liked to get my parents upset with me so they could see my parents yell at me. But what they didn't know was what was going on behind closed doors. It wasn't exactly helpful with the amount of abuse that was going on. I spent a lot of time with those girls. I just wanted to have friends.

As we got older, we all moved away. A couple of us kept in touch. One woman became devoutly religious. When we got together at her father's memorial, she kept apologizing to me for how she treated me when we were growing up. I found out later if she apologized to me three times, she was absolved of her guilt and shame. It didn't matter if I forgave her. All she had to do was repeat her apology three times.

Her sister and I kept in touch maybe once a year. She had moved to the West Coast and would come back to her hometown and try to find the time to get together with her friends. She and I didn't really have a lot in common, but that wasn't a reason not to get together. The last time I saw her was when she was here in 2010. She had very specific plans for each one of her friends. She wanted to meet with me separately. She wanted to go with me to our old neighborhood. She wanted to go out to dinner. Then she wanted me to drop her off to see her cousins.

So she was dropped off at my apartment. I drove us over to our old neighborhood. We talked about a lot of different things. I was pretty candid about the abuse that had been going on in my house. I don't remember her having much of a reaction. I was surprised by that because she was a licensed social worker. I was perplexed by her schedule. But I went with it. We went to dinner. I remember feeling uncomfortable. She seemed a bit self-involved and not very warm and welcoming. Frankly, I was glad when dinner was over. We left the restaurant and got into my car. Honestly, there really was not a lot left to say. I pulled up to our (her) destination and was surprised when she asked me if I wanted to come in and see her cousins. I said sure, that would be nice. I walked in with her. I got a warm welcome. As one of her cousins started to ask me something, she said, "You can go now." I was kind of stunned by how blunt she was. I left and

And it worked. You were liked, had friends, boys liked you and were attracted to you. Of course for more than your looks, but what I'm stressing is this unconscious belief of beauty=safety, lack of beauty=danger was reinforced (and your dad's magazines, I'm sure also fed into this). And so, why I bring this up is now that you're in menopause, I'm sure these unconscious beliefs will be surfacing. Everything that made you (feel) safe is leaving, and with that childhood experience around lack of beauty being dangerous, it would make complete and total sense if you started feeling more scared and afraid in the world without knowing why. Of course, these are just my thoughts—but I wanted to offer them to you as a birthday gift, just in case you've been feeling as such. (Part of why menopause is such Hell is that it brings up all our unconscious (-) beliefs and wounds; even those we thought we healed. - At least that's been my experience.)

Wishing you a year of great joy and a Happy (52nd) Birthday,

love,
[keeping her name anonymous]

I had to read it twice. I cried then got mad. But it hit me it wasn't my imagination that these kids were really mean to me. They were bullies. The other thing that occurred to me was in her point number two, she wasn't talking about me. She was talking about herself. What a nice "birthday gift." I haven't spoken to, e-mailed, or seen her since. I don't need to. She is yet another person who has assigned me a role she needs me to be in, but doesn't know me at all. More importantly, doesn't want to know me as I really am.

The ex-wife of my then-husband was friends with one of the mean girls. This ex-wife and I were very friendly. We spent a lot of time together. It was very adult. The ex-wife, the mean girl, and I all graduated from the same high school class. Our ten-year reunion was the year after I got married. The night of the reunion, my then-husband and I hired the sitter for the kids. We all went to the reunion. I realized that no one had changed that much in ten years. Cliques were still cliques. Mean girls were still mean. In fact, they wanted to start fights, physical and otherwise. I had to get out of there. So my then-husband and I left. The next day the ex-wife called and talked to my then husband. He said I SHOULD talk to her. So I did. Evidently, the mean girl that I had called years before for that heart-to-heart talk called her. She wanted to warn the ex-wife that I was sick and blamed her (the mean girl) for everything that had gone wrong in my life, and I was a danger to the kids. The first thing I remember was seeing my hair start to shake. I lowered my voice and said to the ex-wife, "You know better than to believe any of that. I would throw myself in front of a moving truck rather than let anything happen to your kids." I was furious she would have to check to see if any of that was true. We had been dealing with each other and spending time with each other for a couple of years by then. I went into a dark place in my head. I sat in the dark and didn't speak at home for two weeks. I would only lighten up when I was at work. Everything went back to normal when the ex-wife apologized. But can you imagine someone interjecting themselves that way? What for? To cause trouble, to belittle and humiliate me? Oh yeah, "mean girls"…high school…Some people just don't grow up. I look at it this way: some people peak in high school and have an inability to move forward or mature.

At the thirty-year reunion, the mean girls were together. Honestly, they weren't even very respectful of each other. It was kind of funny. Two of the mean girls were standing together watching me talk to the other ex-wife (by now I had been long divorced). I told you she and I liked each other, respected each other, with the exception of a couple of weeks after the ten-year reunion. We were standing together talking about the kids. The next thing I knew, these two

told him I hadn't lost any sleep over it, but I thought it would be a good thing for me to let him know how I felt about it. As he was about to say something, a drunk woman (a mean girl associate) decided to come over and literally drape herself over me and say a big slurred "hi" to me. Mr. Famous Author asked her to give us a minute because we were talking. She made her stumbling exit. So back to what he said; he sort of apologized. He didn't have much recollection of the encounter. For me, it didn't matter what he remembered. As we were talking, he had a hand in his pocket, and a drink in the other hand. He pulled his hand out of his pocket and out fell a tape recorder. It slid across the floor. He became very nervous, almost panic-stricken. He assured me he wasn't taping any of our conversation. In fact, he "assured" me way too much. I was done with what I had to say anyway. So off I went to find my friends I had arrived with.

In grade school I met this cute, funny girl. We became instant friends. She didn't live very far from me. We would ride bikes together, go to each other's houses, even have sleepovers. Even back then my friendships felt deep and important. She and I were seemingly inseparable. We were extremely close in junior high as well. In fact, we were friends all through school and continued our close friendship after we graduated from high school. I loved her so much.

Around the time I started having my anxiety disorder and subsequent agoraphobia, it was tough for me to get out and around, especially by myself. When I was housebound, people would come over to visit. It wasn't an easy time to say the least. My friend had met someone and gotten engaged. She was excitedly planning her wedding. Of course I would shore myself up to be able to go to her wedding! I didn't think anything would or could keep me away. In fact, I had someone take me shopping to buy a dress so I would be ready for the big day. I was happy and excited for her.

About a month before her wedding, she called me. She wanted to know if I could meet her at a restaurant near my apartment. Being agoraphobic, as hard as that was going to be, I agreed to meet her. I got dressed, hyperventilated, and left my apartment to go to my car. It was all I could do to leave my home. Between my home and the restaurant there were railroad tracks. In my agoraphobic state, those

had been working there for a while. She was very happy with her life. One day at work she had gone into the women's bathroom and into one of the stalls. The door to the stall had somehow detached and fell on her head. She had been injured and diagnosed with a traumatic brain injury. While in the hospital, she started to suffer with a panic disorder and agoraphobia. This injury changed her whole life. Somewhere in all of her suffering, she realized what I had been going through. What she had said about me being "far too depressing to be around" when referring to me years earlier, she now knew what it was like and she owed me an apology for being so uncaring and judgmental. I just stared at her. I told her how sorry I was that had happened to her. Most importantly, I wanted her to know I would never have wished that on her or anyone for that matter. After that, I don't remember anything else from that meeting. It could have been my PTSD that had me tune out for the rest of the time, or maybe other things were just too painful to remember. I know I got home just fine. That was the last time I heard from her, which really is OK by me. I want to say karma is a bitch, but do I really feel that way? Not really. Well…

Fourth Grade: I liked my teacher a lot but was also leery around her. She laughed at students. Not in the laugh-with-you sense but a belittling laugh-at-you way. I wanted her to like me. She made fun of the way I kept the inside of my desk. She called me "Pig Pen" in front of the other kids. They laughed. I took it to heart. I heard it as I was "Pig Pen." Many years later she was my stepson's fourth-grade teacher. She had married and changed her last name. But I would have recognized her anywhere.

Fifth Grade: The teacher seemed much older than the others. Certainly more old-fashioned. She kicked me out of a spelling bee because she thought I was using sign language to help another student spell a word. I wasn't, but I had to sit down anyway.

Sixth Grade: Was traumatic. The teacher was loud, obnoxious, and cruel. He would make sure to single students out and tell them they were stupid in front of the whole class. He did that to me once, and I started crying uncontrollably. A very brave sixth-grade student stood up and told him to leave me alone (that person is a Rabbi now). This teacher would read poetry and pound his fists on the desks of students. It was all quite frightening. His behavior was so odd. You just never knew what he was going to do next. Would he yell, would he tell a joke, lie to us about textbooks not being available, rant, belittle? Which personality would show up for class each day? I was terrified every day. Again, I was mostly terrified of everything all of the time.

Years later I was told he had died of liver failure. He had a terrible drinking problem for years. Well, that explained everything. Explained, but didn't excuse him for his behavior.

I noticed a big difference between fifth and sixth grade. Kids were meaner, more judgmental, and cruel. I don't know why, but things got so much harder for me. I thought maybe junior high would be different. Oh, how wrong I would be.

have to be at every practice, even though I probably wouldn't dance. I had to know all of the girls' dance steps in case I had to sub for them if someone was sick. There were four or five alternates, one for every unit. Some of the time the alternates went to games even if they weren't subbing for someone. I think my favorite (insert sarcasm) story would be…I was at a college football game where the dance line was dancing. I was watching from the stands. It "appeared" that one of the girls got woozy and had to be taken off the sidelines. I was asked to sub for her. I had no costumes of my own. Alternates were not allowed to buy any. So I had to put this girl's sweaty costume on and sub for her. I can still remember how it felt to put on that wet, sweaty, smelly sequined costume. It sends shivers down my spine thinking about how gross it was. Turns out, she was hungover and didn't feel like dancing anymore. She didn't know that I heard her tell someone that. But that was my job as an alternate. It was what was expected. What I SHOULD do. That wouldn't be the first or last time that would happen. So I figured I'd automatically be made a full-fledged dance line member when tryouts came around. Nope. They made all the alternates try out all over again. My friends tried out with me. None of us made it in. Not even me! I wanted to know why. I called the director of the dance line, and she told me, "After speaking with all of the girls, they thought you acted like you were a full-fledged member instead of an alternate." I was hurt and shocked! I was also told that because I didn't drop all of my outside friends, I wasn't wanted in the group. What kind of person would I have been if I could easily have dropped my real friends?

That's how tenth grade started for me. That was followed up by people from the dance line group, who I thought were my friends, not being allowed to talk to me anymore. So every day I saw these people, every day they dismissed me with their eyes and attitudes. Welcome to high school. Some of these were the "mean girls," and the "mean girls" just got meaner. It was painful. They weren't just "mean girls" to me, but to a lot of people. Before there was a movie called *The Mean Girls,* it was a reality at our high school from 1975 to 1977. After hearing about the movie when it came out in 2004, I realized it was a universal theme.

paper declaring myself an adult. When I didn't want to be in school, I would write myself a note and bring it to the office. It usually said, "I don't feel like being here today. Sincerely, Roberta." The school couldn't do anything about it. I was eighteen in December, school ended in June. I was considered an adult at eighteen. I'm not sure how I managed to graduate, but I guess I must have done enough work and showed up just enough. My grades in high school were Bs and Cs. I was so glad to be done with high school.

Long before there was Columbine, I would have a recurring daydream about being shot in the hallway at school. The daydream involved getting shot on the way to or from the bathroom or on my way to a class. I would be the only one in the hallway, except the shooter. I would be shot in the upper arm, and the shooter would run out of the school. The daydream would continue with people taking care of me and being nice to me. What an odd way to daydream about getting positive attention or what I believed at that time would be positive attention. Reflecting on it now, it wouldn't have been positive attention. It would have been people feeling sorry for me. Of course, I never ever told anyone about my daydream. Not then for sure. I'm just talking about it now. It makes me shake my head how lost I was as a young girl. How lost I would stay for a long time.

I wanted to go to college after I graduated. I wanted to be an English teacher. But I studied the statistics of how likely it would be that I would find a job teaching English after graduating from college. The numbers weren't good. The numbers said there would be a glut of English teachers and not enough jobs to go around. So I opted out of going to college and kept my job selling shoes. I worked retail for years until my anxiety disorder and agoraphobia made it impossible for me to work. I went to therapy as my new "job." I was on disability for a while. When I started seeing the light at the end of the tunnel, and it wasn't the light from an oncoming train, I started to venture out of my house. I decided I was going to go to cosmetology school to get my manicurist license. There was a school not too far from where I was living. I drove up there and got all the information about courses, tuition, and loans. After thinking about it for a few days, I enrolled. I was terrified. I hadn't really left

---------— CHAPTER 9 ——————

Boys to Men
The Relationships

My first real date happened when I was fifteen. I had gone to a New Year's party with a friend and was introduced to him. He was so cute. He asked me if I would go out with him to a movie the following week. I told him I had to talk to my parents about it. Whenever the topic of dating came up at home, my folks said I couldn't date until I was sixteen. I don't know why, but when I asked them, they said it would be OK. So the following week, he and I double-dated with our friends. I was dressed in nice dark green corduroy pants and a soft, green argyle patterned sweater. Brand new, of course. I was wearing a mid-length navy blue wool coat. Good thing I had that coat on because we stood in line outside for quite some time to see *The Exorcist*. I had read the book; how much scarier could the movie be? Oh, my naiveté. I was so terrified during the movie I think I watched most of it through my fingers while I covered my face. I had never seen anything like that before. I was so scared I felt sick. But I didn't want to be a baby, so I sat through the whole thing. The guys thought the movie was funny and fakey, or so they said. I don't remember my girlfriend saying much of anything. I can tell you that I didn't sleep well for months. After

and told him it hurt. He assured me we were "almost there." I felt myself chickening out. It hurt too much. I told him how much it hurt. The next thing I knew, he put a pillow over my face and forced himself inside me. It was excruciating! I was crying. He held me and when he was done he told me it would get easier. All I kept thinking was, is this what everyone is talking about? I didn't realize what truly had just happened. I thought the first time for everyone was like that. Remember, I was scared of everything all of the time. But I knew I had made him happy. Wasn't that why we were together? Isn't that what I SHOULD have done? We continued to have sex. I continued to read up on different techniques. I asked him one day why he didn't go down on me? I had certainly done that for him. He answered me totally straight-faced, "Eww, that's just gross." It was never talked about again. Several months later I skipped a period. I was scared, and I SHOULD have been. In 1976, I was pregnant in high school. What was I going to do? I talked to my boyfriend about it, and he thought I must have been mistaken. He took me to a clinic for a pregnancy test. I was not mistaken. I should add here that I have found my journals from 1975 to 1976 so all of this was documented. I was taking Forkner Shorthand in school and everything I wanted to hide from my parents I wrote in shorthand. Forty years after writing it, I can still read it. So now we had to face some kind of decision. According to my journal and my memory, he said, "I can always deny it's mine because you've got a reputation." Wow! How could I have a reputation if he was the only person I had been with?

A week or so after learning I was pregnant, a bunch of us went on a ski trip. I had terrible morning sickness (all day). Skiing was not my top priority. Making a decision and keeping that decision from my parents was critical. Regardless of the circumstance, on that ski trip my boyfriend woke me up at 4:00 a.m. to have sex, where I promptly quoted Elton John, "It's four in the morning dammit, listen to me good." We decided I would have an abortion. Luckily (for lack of a better word) that was the first year a girl of sixteen or seventeen didn't need parental consent. If my parents would have found out, they would have sent me away for sure. What was required by law was four hours of counseling: individual, group, birth-control

A few months ago I had coffee with my first serious boyfriend, the man who took my virginity. He is now an attorney. I wanted to let him know I was writing a book about my life. I assured him I wasn't using any names. Attorneys make me nervous. They're so… so…litigious!

I did my share of dating in high school. I had a couple of boyfriends I slept with. It seemed like the thing to do. It also seemed empowering for me. I didn't really understand why. It was a fun thing to do and made me happy, for lack of a better term.

Another high school romance was what I would call a trophy romance. He was handsome, popular, funny, and drove a nice car. I also thought he could be "the one." What did I know? I was seventeen. We had a lot of fun together. We went to lots of high school parties where I did my fair share of underage drinking. One of the most memorable nights, we were at this party and I started drinking Everclear (100% vodka) topped off with a little lemonade just to make the liquor go down easier. I don't know where my boyfriend was while I was getting totally smashed, but I know someone went to get him when I fell into the kitchen sink. I had been sitting on the kitchen counter, got drunk, and fell into the sink. He came in to the kitchen and told me it was probably time to leave. I walked outside with him and lay down on the grass. I wouldn't get up until he promised I could drive his car. I know! We were so young and so foolish. Both of us, because he let me drive myself home. He helped me out of the car, got me inside (thankfully my parents were out for the evening) and got me into my room. The next thing I knew, it was the middle of the night, and I was still in my clothes from the party. I got up, put on pajamas, brushed my teeth, realized I was still drunk, got into bed, and fell asleep. I woke up around 8:00 a.m. It was Sunday and I had to go to the synagogue where I was an assistant teacher. Problem…I was still a little tipsy. There was no way I could call in sick without alerting my parents that I had been drinking. So off I went to teach. I also had a job at a retail clothing store that I had to be at. It was a very long day.

Getting back to the boyfriend part of this, I really liked him. I don't remember how long we were together, I think only a few

relationship was "the one." But I really thought he was "the one" for sure. We got along really well, except for an argument we had in Civics class. We were on opposite sides of the issue, and it got heated. It carried over into our relationship. In fact, I wrote a not-so-flattering story about him in my Moffett class. But we worked things out. Just a funny side note, he and I are still friends, and one day we were talking about this Civics class incident. I referenced myself as his girlfriend back then. We had dated for about a year and a half. He told me he never thought of me as his girlfriend. Isn't that interesting? Kind of funny. I always thought he was my boyfriend for that year and a half. Go figure. But I digress. In all the time we went out, we only slept together once. We got really high, and he put on the long disco version of Donna Summer's "Love to Love You Baby" on the record player. Now why would I think I was his girlfriend? That summer he went away to work at a camp. Our high school romance was done.

After my dad had nearly beaten me to death and I ran away, I ended up at my new boyfriend's college dorm. We then moved out of his dorm and found an apartment where we would become caretakers. Not my choice of a job, but where else was I going to go? My impression was this guy was going to take care of me. He was completely horrified by the beating I took from my dad. All I knew was I couldn't live with my parents, not with as terrified as I was of my father. I continued to go to high school, and I wanted to graduate. So caretaker by night, high schooler by day. There was a lot of talk at school about me living with my boyfriend. But I never discussed it with anyone except my best friend. The day of my graduation this guy and I got into an argument. I don't remember what it was about, but I can tell you we were in his car. We were driving down the highway yelling at each other. He pulled over to the shoulder, stopped the car, and told me to get out. So I got out. He drove away leaving me on the highway. I had to get back to the apartment to get my cap and gown. So I started walking. From then on it's blank until the actual graduation ceremony. I stood with the rest of the class before we were ushered to our chairs. People were passing joints and laughing.

Years later I ran into the woman who was in the bathroom with me that night. She had to reintroduce herself to me. I didn't remember her. She wanted to ask me something about that night. She wanted to know how I pulled myself together and went out that night. I was stunned. I said, "We went out?" She told me that not only did we go to dinner, but we went to a movie too. I told her I had no recollection past she and I in the bathroom together. I couldn't even tell her when or how the relationship ended. If I'm not mistaken, I moved back to my parents after he and I broke up.

My next relationship was truly the one that got away, my own fault, really. I met him at the apartment complex I was living at. He was the maintenance guy when I was the caretaker. We had become friends. We didn't start dating until several months after my breakup. He was sweet, kind, funny, self-sufficient, easy to talk to, and easy to be with. He was like the Patrick Swayze character in *Dirty Dancing*, sweet and sensitive, with a wild—but not too wild—side. He drove a 1956 Belvedere. He loved that car. He had a motorcycle too. He wasn't like anyone else I had ever dated. Best thing, he liked me for me. We fell madly in love. Of course, my parents disapproved. At one point my mother threw herself up against the front door and wouldn't let me go outside where he was waiting for me. She said I couldn't go out with him because he was "no more than a janitor." (Ironically, he became a school janitor in another state when he moved away and married his high school sweetheart). I didn't understand what that meant for her. For me, it meant he had a job he liked, a life he liked and was a responsible adult. After I peeled her off the door, I joined him in his '56 Belvedere and off we went to dinner and a movie. He and I moved in together several months later.

It was a great, healthy relationship. We were so happy. We lived together for quite a while and started talking about getting married. He wasn't sold on the idea but said he would think about it. We became engaged about three months later. I don't know what happened to me. I started thinking maybe this wasn't a good idea. He was great! He took care of me when I was sick and vice versa. He was creative, he was an artist, he was responsible. He was gorgeous and best of all, he wasn't violent. I became uneasy, distracted, then…I

gerous, and of course the one I fell in love with was, well, let's just call him "D" for Dangerous. D was intense, he was handsome, he was funny at times. He had tattoos and a barrel chest. He fascinated me. He was really good at getting me to do just about anything. I'd drive him to his strip shows or private parties and pick him up afterward. At one point he moved in with me. He really didn't have much stuff—a gym bag full of clothes and a shaving kit. He smoked pot; sometimes I would smoke with him. He took different kinds of pills like quaaludes, brown and clears, tranquilizers, none of which I was interested in trying. He was really into shooting up crystal meth and sometimes heroin or coke. He was drug addicted. This was a real compromise to how I lived. He would shoplift to support his habit. He'd even have me come along. This was not how I lived my life. But I "loved" him.

One day he wanted to borrow my car, and I let him. He didn't come back for what I think was two days. I had to go out searching. I had a good idea where he might be. And there was my car, in front of his ex-girlfriend's house. I had my extra set of keys and took my car back. He got a ride over to my house and apologized, asked me to forgive him. He said it wouldn't happen again. Then everything changed. He became horribly violent. The first time he beat me up I ended up in the emergency room. I heard myself say, "I fell down the stairs." He came over and of course he apologized and begged me to take him back. He explained how it had happened, and he would make sure it would never happen again. You know all those Lifetime movies where you can't believe that a woman takes a man back after he beats her? D and I were on and off for four years. But not how you would think. The very last time he beat me up, he nearly broke my arm while whipping me into a wall. Something tore under my shoulder blade. In fact, it is an injury that flares up to this day, as well as others he inflicted. He managed to give me herpes in the time that we were together. There is nothing like not being able to forget an old relationship. But I consider myself lucky that's all I contracted from him, especially being he was an intravenous drug user.

I finally filed a restraining order against him. He would break the order by showing up at my work or breaking into my apartment.

him his manicure. He went up to pay at the register, and he realized he forgot his wallet. I laughed at him and teased him about trying to get a freebie. I told him not to worry about it. Later that day a huge bouquet of roses arrived with a card apologizing and asking me out for the following week. How romantic! I said yes. We had dated for a few weeks when he agreed to come to my last court date regarding my ex-boyfriend. It was nice to have him there dressed in a suit, looking like an attorney. I felt protected. Even though I was still having terrible nightmares about D, I was ready to move forward in my life.

I was renting the basement of a house when we started dating. It was not ideal, but it did keep me out of the elements. About a month after we started dating, he was supposed to spend the night but he didn't show up. I couldn't imagine where he was. He called the next day as if nothing was wrong. I reminded him he said he was going to spend the night. I told him I had even powdered the sheets with his favorite perfume of mine…Raffinee. With an, "Oh, my G-d, I'm sorry, but the guys and I were playing poker and I spaced it out. Will you forgive me?" He promised to make it up to me. I forgave him.

We dated about six months before we started house hunting. I was spending nights at his apartment if his kids weren't there. We spent a lot of time together. It seemed like the logical next step. Our house hunting went on for about a month. Then we found the cutest three-bedroom rambler across the street from a small lake. We later found out it was called "A lake with a ponding area." We put a bid in on it, and with some negotiating we got it! He called me at work to let me know. We went to dinner to celebrate. He was telling me about the negotiations. He was very proud to admit that, "If they don't call you an asshole when the negotiating was done, then you left money on the table." I thought he was kidding and didn't think much of it. I now know those are the things you pay attention to.

About a month later we moved into our home. We had some new carpeting put in, had some redecorating and cleaning to do. But it really felt like ours. We had done it up in art-deco style. Pretty severe, but tasteful, black lacquer furniture, rose-colored carpeting, black couch and chair in the living room. The den was more kid friendly, vinyl couch, easy to clean. That was the family room. The

a blindfold on his chair. He looked at me and said, "What's this?" I told him…dinner. So he changed into something more comfortable and sat down at the table. I proceeded to tie his hands behind his back and put the blindfold on him. I promised there were no tricks or pranks, just dinner. I had all kinds of dipping sauces and meats, as well as his cocktail. It was all very sexy! When he said he was done eating, I led him downstairs and popped in the movie. Again, very sexy until…he took a pair of scissors and cut my brand new lingerie off of me. But, I wasn't going to let that ruin the evening. I went with it. We made love and watched the movie. It was quite an evening, if I do say so myself. When the movie was over, we walked upstairs. He opened the pocket doors and saw the kitchen. He started yelling at me about how messy the kitchen was. How could I leave pots and pans in the sink? Why didn't I clean this up before he got home? I stood there agog. I couldn't even speak. He decided to go to bed. I cleaned up the kitchen. My head was swimming. I just kept asking myself, how could he be so insensitive and unappreciative? I couldn't believe it. I stayed up and thought carefully about what I wanted to do next.

He woke up at his usual time to get ready for work. I didn't have much to say. He left for work. I called my mom and asked her if I could move back in until I found a place of my own. I packed all of my clothes, shoes, makeup, and anything that belonged just to me, and loaded my car and drove to my parents' house. Not exactly the game plan I had in mind, but it was only temporary.

He came home from work to find me and my stuff gone. I think I left a note for him explaining how hurt I was and how unappreciated I felt, that I had to think it through regarding our relationship. He drove over to my parents' house and we sat outside talking. I was crying. I really had been devastated. Of course he apologized. He wanted me to come back home. I told him I needed time to think. It took me a few days and lots of talking, but I moved back to our house. He promised nothing like that would ever happen again. I believed him. *Oy!*

We went back to getting along. He made an effort to be more sensitive. We settled into being together, being in love with each

tial dinner was beautiful. I was very emotional. Relatives flew in from all over the country. It was lovely. The wedding was the next day. My parents stayed at the hotel with my relatives who flew in, leaving me to be able to stay at their house with my maid of honor and away from my husband-to-be. In retrospect, that seems silly because the limo picked us up at our house, and we rode together to the synagogue. Oh well. I got in the limo and said I had forgotten something. I ran back in our house and put up a "Just Married" sign on the wall behind our bed. Then it was off to have pictures taken.

We arrived, and the bridesmaids and I were in one room, the guys in another. I had my Janet Jackson cassette playing so we could dance around. We all got ready to meet with the photographer. He was a friend of mine for years, and I trusted whatever he wanted to do. He wanted to get a picture of me pinning a flower on my beloved's lapel. I took the flower out of the box; my beloved snatched it out of my hand, pulled the "greens" off the back of the flower, and said, "I told you, I just wanted a flower, no greens." That was news to me. But we got the picture and continued posing, etcetera. His usher friend thought it was fun and funny to unzip my wedding dress while we were standing side-by-side in a group photo. I made the best of the antics. The time had come; we were to line up to walk down the aisle. First my sister and his brother, then my maid of honor and his best man, then the boys in their rented tuxes and black tennis shoes. Then it was my turn. My mother was on one side of me, my father on the other. Just as the harpist started playing "Always," by Atlantic Starr, the photographer ran up the aisle straight at me. He pushed me by my chest with his hand and said, "My camera just broke. Wait here. I have another one in my car." And there I stood with people wondering why I wasn't moving. I heard the door open and there was the photographer motioning me forward. It really wasn't more than a few minutes. But it was interesting. After the ceremony, my sister told me she thought I'd run out the back door. Kind of funny, but not really my MO.

We stood under the chuppah (Jewish bridal canopy) as our Rabbi talked to us. My uncle, also a Rabbi, took part in marrying us too. It was lovely. It felt warm and welcoming. I looked over and

I don't know. I will admit in retrospect that he and I may have been twenty-six and twenty-seven, but I don't think either one of us knew what actual marriage entailed. He, being married before, told me it was going to be different for him this time. But I don't believe we had the maturity or understanding of how to make a relationship work.

I just want to lay the framework for what I found shocking and hurtful. We had been married just a couple of weeks. We had gotten into bed and started to make love. At least that's what I thought we were doing. In the middle of the act, he says to me, "You're my whore, my own personal whore." He had never said anything like that to me before. I started to cry and said, "I'm not your whore, I'm your wife." I cried and cried. I couldn't figure out where that came from. Why he thought he had the right to say something so awful and demeaning to me. From that night forward, I found him repulsive. But I was his wife, and I SHOULD have sex with him, right? It was all I could do to feign interest. But I performed my wifely duty, until I couldn't stomach it anymore. The days/nights that he would want to have sex and I said no, he would put a red "X" on the calendar that hung in the kitchen. After a couple of weeks of the "Xs," the kids asked him what the Xs were for. He answered, "Ask Roberta." I don't remember what I said to them when they asked, or even if I addressed it at all. I just knew we weren't going to be OK. That first year was difficult, but we kept it together, sort of.

About three years into the marriage, he was traveling for business a lot. He would come home, and we would have sex. Lather, rinse, repeat. I started not feeling well. I had what seemed to be some sort of odd, severe yeast infection. It just wouldn't go away. I finally went to the doctor and was diagnosed with gardnerella, a sexually transmitted disease. I wasn't having sex with anyone else; hell, I was hardly having sex with my husband. I suddenly remembered a conversation we had while dating. He said hookers didn't count as cheating. I went blank. I never mentioned it to anyone.

Five and a half years went by, and I realized I had had enough of the dysfunction. What kept me hanging in there was my love for his kids and my love for his parents. But was it enough? The kids had already been through one divorce; how would they handle another?

me. What a terrible person I was to ask them to go separately. I was emotionally shut down. He continued yelling at me all the way to the synagogue. He pulled up at the door and told me to get out while he parked the car. Really? He was going to let me walk in by myself? In all my numbness, I put one foot in front of the other and walked through the door where I promptly got light-headed and collapsed. Luckily a couple of people caught me before I hit the ground and brought me into the "family room." The next thing I remember was sitting next to my dad in the front pew as he held his "Battle of Midway" hat. He said he brought it with because if he could survive the sinking of the Yorktown in World War II, he could survive this.

After the service my cousin and her husband asked if they could ride with us to the cemetery. They had taken a taxi from the airport and had no car. I was dazed. I must've said yes. All the way to the cemetery my husband kept saying, "Your cousins are good enough to ride with us, but my kids aren't?" I was numb. I do remember seeing the look in my cousin's eyes. But I kept quiet, so did she and her husband.

We got to the cemetery for the graveside service. This is by tradition where relatives can throw dirt on the casket. It's thought of as an honor. To me it was a horror. I couldn't be part of actually burying my mother. I told my husband not to throw dirt either because I knew he didn't like her, and he had made some comment about how it would be his pleasure to help bury her. However he meant it, it made me feel sick. Neither one of us would throw any dirt in.

We drove back home, and I really needed to lie down. The kids had come back with us. I changed out of my clothes while he and the kids were in the kitchen. When I came out, the oldest child started yelling that he hated me. He said I didn't think he was good enough to ride to the funeral with me. He was twelve. Where do you think that notion came from? I was past numb and couldn't even address it. I went to my room and took a nap. A couple of hours later we had to be at my parents' house for the first night of Shiva. I don't think the kids were with us for that. I think they went back to their mother's house. We got there before people showed up for the service. My dad and my sister were having some kind of fight. I didn't know about

where the couch used to be and think about the divorce. I asked my dad if I could move into the basement of his house until I could find a place. He said no. So I ended up moving into a condo with one of my soon-to-be ex-husband's cousins. She was looking for a renter, and she lived in our same neighborhood. My soon-to-be ex wouldn't allow me to take both cats, so they were split up too. He only really liked the one he wanted to keep.

The divorce process was awful. All I wanted to do was get it over with. I didn't fight for any value I had put into the house. His attorney contacted me and offered me two years of alimony. I said fine.

Since we were in the same neighborhood, the kids would ride their bikes over so they could go swimming. I really did love them. One day the youngest was over and told me, "Daddy has a new girlfriend, and I think it's too soon, and it makes my stomach hurt." I asked him if he talked to his daddy about it. He said no. I told him he needed to say something to his daddy or mommy. I didn't need to know what was going on with his dad, but it was good that he told somebody.

After the youngest left, I called his dad. He became furious! All I said was that the youngest needed to talk to him about his girlfriend. He hung up on me. The next call I got was from the kid's mom. She and I had always gotten along. But she was furious as well. She was yelling at me about "pumping her kids for information." Never. I didn't want to take furniture so they wouldn't feel bad. Why would I do such an awful thing to them? She told me to never have contact with her kids again. I was floored. So that ended me seeing the kids unless we were at the grocery store at the same time. It didn't happen often, but it happened.

A few weeks later my soon-to-be ex called and asked me to give back his mother's Passover recipes. I told him I would copy them, but I would like a few of her original recipe cards. He blew up and hung up on me. The next thing I know the phone rings, and it was the oldest son calling and asking for his grandmother's recipes. I told him no problem. I would make copies so we could all have them, and I would drop them off. He said, "No, you'll give us all of the originals because you're not family, and you don't count anymore."

didn't cover when we had to meet for our Ghet (Jewish Divorce). We had to do some ritualistic walking around each other so we could be divorced in Israel. The regular divorce was official, but honestly, I didn't want us to be on record as being married anywhere, including Israel. When all the rituals were done, it was official. We were divorced…everywhere.

I got in my car and totally broke down crying. It was just too much. In five months we had lost his mom, his aunt, our dog, my mother, and our marriage. Yes, I said five months. It was overwhelming. He came up to the window of my car and knocked. He asked me if I was OK. Did I want to come over and talk, and I did. It was really over, thank G-d. By the way, he married that woman he was seeing. They've since divorced. He's now looking for ex-wife no. 4. In fact, when my dad died, he was calling me from another state trying to convince me to get back together. It was only a few weeks, and I realized he hadn't changed a bit, but I had. I could see his BS from two thousand miles away.

Although I wasn't divorced yet, I was trying to move on with my life. I had met someone, and we were just beginning to date. I was returning a movie to the video store, and I heard someone call my name. I turned around and there was the former manager of a salon I worked at. We stood and talked for a while. It was nice to catch up with him. He was probably one of the most handsome men I had ever seen. I was walking away, and he asked me if I would like to go out to dinner when he got back from his trip. I said yes, and we exchanged phone numbers. I was pretty excited. I hadn't been out on a date in a long time. My divorce was almost final. The timing was good. He called me from out of town. I was thrilled! And so began our relationship. He took me out to dinner. He was such a gentleman. He made me laugh; he brought me flowers once a week. I liked that he wasn't rushing me into bed. I liked this "slow moving, getting to know each other" thing.

A few months went by. He was in and out of town traveling for business. I got a call one night, and he said when he got back he'd like to sit down and have a talk. I said sure. I got off the phone and tried to figure out what that was all about. I narrowed it down to

I thought it was sweet that he decided to get allergy shots so he could be around my cats.

It was about three months into the relationship, and everything was going smoothly. One night we went to the hospital to see a friend of mine. Afterward I dropped him off at his apartment. He said he was tired, and I had plans to go out with a girlfriend. I'm not sure if we were saying the "love" word yet, but I certainly let him know that I cared about him. I called him before I went out and there was no answer. I figured he must have been in the shower or something. My girlfriend and I went out as planned and got home about 1:30 a.m. I checked for messages on my voice mail and found a peculiar message from "my man." He was saying something about me not being where I said I would be. After listening to the message, I realized he was drunk. So begins the downward slide. I called him back, and he started accusing me of the craziest things. What was I doing—or should he rephrase—"who" was I doing? Why I would take it upon myself to try to talk sense into someone three sheets to the wind is beyond me. I guess it's that training I've referred to before. I thought I could fix things. There really wasn't anything to be fixed, but I was going to fix it. I actually tried to talk sense into him until 4:00 a.m. I finally realized he wasn't sobering up at all; it just seemed to get worse. I told him I wasn't going to discuss it anymore, and we would talk at a later date.

I went to bed for a few hours, then got going early that morning. I had turned my mobile phone on in case someone needed me while I was running errands. My phone rang. Guess who? He wanted to know if I was still talking to him. I told him I wasn't very happy, and I was not up to dealing with this kind of problem. He said he needed to talk to me in person. I agreed to meet him for lunch. Sheepish is an understatement. I've never seen a man so sorry. I told him in no uncertain terms how I felt about drug and alcohol problems and was not up to dealing with it. Been there, done that! He said it wouldn't happen again. The problem, as I saw it, was not just the fact he went out drinking, he went out drinking alone and drove home drunk. I wasn't very fond of the tone he took with me, nor the accusations he made when he left me the voice mail. He kept apologizing. I asked

for I can't remember how long. You'd think a person would learn. This was not the first time in the workhouse for the same reason. When he got out, he couldn't drive anywhere. If I wanted to see him, I had to go pick him up, unless he was being stubborn and insisted on walking in the below zero temperatures. Oh, well, maybe something would teach him a lesson.

When I saw him the first night after he got out of the workhouse, all he did was tell me how uncomfortable the pillows were, how bad the food was, and how loud and strange the people were in jail. I told him I couldn't feel very sorry for him because it wasn't supposed to be a five-star hotel. Can you say, "On the way to a breakup"? We're coming into the final stretch of the last straw. Now the two of us had more problems than this. I will be the first to admit I expect respect and if I don't get it, I lose patience really easily. I give respect; I SHOULD get respect, right? Fat chance. That is the thing dreams are made of. Back to the story.

I went to pick him up one night so he could come over for a while. He was kind of pissy in the car, but I chose to ignore it. We got back to the house and cuddled up on the couch. Things were strained but seemed to be getting better. We ended up in bed trying to make love. I had to be very specific; he was very distant but interested. That probably doesn't make any sense, but that's the way it was. He was standing behind me, I could see him in the mirror, and the strangest thing came to mind. He looked like a perfect crescent moon. I couldn't get that thought out of my mind during this short-lived encounter. When he was done he said, "Is that what you wanted?" As if this was all my idea. After that statement, I told him I would take him home, knowing that was the last time we would be together. The good thing about that relationship was I found out I could have deep feelings for someone or something other than my cats.

In my twenties, I discovered my sexual freedom. I could have sex with abandon. No judgments, just adventure. I had anxiety about so many things. Sex was not one of them. I became experienced, whatever that means. I thought everyone felt that sex was a way of expressing yourself, relieving tension, blowing off steam, if you will. Not necessarily an "intimacy." As I've said, sex was challenging in my

and make it up to me. SHOULDN'T I give him a second chance? Of course I SHOULD.

We continued to see each other for another six months or so. Every time we had sex, I doubted that sex was supposed to be fun anymore. Maybe we were "at an age" that sex isn't fun? How is that possible? At that six-month mark, he took me to a party where people were watching college basketball championships. His friends seemed nice enough. I wasn't a basketball fan and ended up talking to some women in the kitchen who didn't care if they saw the game either. It was a nice evening. Two days later he broke up with me totally out of the blue. I was shocked! He told me he had to break up with me because he was ashamed and embarrassed to bring me around his friends because he didn't know how to explain me. I had not gone to college and that seemed to be a problem for him. The other problem was that I didn't have any money. What? So he came over and got what few things he had left at my place. But he thought it would be nice if he gave me his Basia CD. So the moral of this story is: Sex is supposed to be fun and compatible. Some men are shallow and idiots. But on the up side, I have Basia CD—really the best thing about the whole relationship…sad, but true. By the way, he went on to marry an attorney. Evidently she had the appropriate credentials. I wish them well.

It would be many years before I would get into another relationship. They hadn't served me very well in the past. Why do it again? Out of the blue, I started thinking about this guy I met when I was in junior high. We had run into each other in various places around the city for years and years. Every time we'd see each other, one or both of us would be involved in a relationship, or one or both of us were married. I started wondering what happened to him. I called his cousin. His cousin told me he was single and living in Arizona. SHOULD I dare call him? Of course I SHOULD. I got his voice mail. I left a message. Within a day I heard back. He seemed very happy to hear from me. We started talking every day, sometimes twice a day. He told me he was thinking about moving back here soon. He just had to work out some things about the custody of his son with his ex-wife. Months went by, and he decided to fly up to see

for him was focused on why he couldn't fly. I told him to call his five-year-old son and explain to him that the President of the United States said he couldn't fly home. That was the best explanation he could give. For four days he paced and carried on. I understood the frustration of not being able to do what he needed to do, but this was a national security issue. I remember thinking the silence of no planes flying over was deafening. Finally, the ban was lifted, and he flew back to Arizona to start preparing for his move here. It was hard to gauge my anxiety. It seemed to match up with the country's anxiety. I don't think I could have put the pieces together of how significant his reaction was to not being able to leave.

Several weeks later, we began our life together. I had a two-bedroom, one-bathroom condo in the suburbs. It was a little tough integrating his stuff in with mine, but I was more than happy to do it. We settled in nicely together. We spent time with his and my friends. Just about everyone loved us together. A couple of my friends were a little skeptical, but they went with it. He was quite charming, sweet, and funny. I felt I was in the healthiest relationship I had ever been in. We seemed to communicate really well. We did all those "couple" things together. We went to the coffee shop on Sunday morning before we would go shopping at Costco. We met friends for dinners and breakfasts. We worked hard at our respective jobs. I seemed to be paying a little bit more than he was, but for me that was OK until he got settled.

About a year went by, and he came home from work and wanted to talk. We sat down on the couch, and he told me he felt really bad that he wasn't contributing enough financially to our household. He thought maybe he should move out so he wouldn't be a burden. As odd as I thought that statement was, I assured him he wasn't a burden and that I was sure work for him would pick up. I wasn't worried. He asked me if I was sure. I said, of course. That's what couples do, support each other during tough times.

We continued to live together in what I thought was a happy relationship. My engagement ring was ready, so we went together to pick it up. It was beautiful. It was gold and the crown was made of hearts that the diamond set into. I showed my ring to my sister and

behaving that way. He had no answer. He told me he was going to bed. He went into our room and closed the door and promptly went to sleep. I, on the other hand, stayed up all night with a yellow legal pad divided into two columns, one "pro," one "con." I wrote down things in both columns, but the "con" column won.

As soon as the clock struck 9:00 a.m., I went in to our room, woke him up, and told him he had to move out. I told him we SHOULD continue to talk to the counselor. Maybe separately we could work things out. But I would not allow anyone to throw something at my head and treat me so disrespectfully. He got up, took his time, called his friends, and arranged to move his stuff, including the dresser I bought for him. By that night, he was gone. By that night, I was heartbroken.

We continued to talk on the phone every other day. The strange thing was, I wanted to work things out; he just wanted me to buy him things. Our counseling appointment was coming up, and he agreed to go, at least one last time. While we were in session I said to the psychologist, "Either he is bipolar, or he is a con man." The psychologist asked me why I had to "label" what was happening. I said, "Because my behavior hasn't changed at all, his has." He became angry. She tried to get him to talk about his anger but to no avail.

About two weeks later his cellular phone bill arrived. I looked at the outside of the envelope and then threw it on the floor. I stared at it for hours. I finally somehow rationalized in my head that I was paying for his phone, and because it was on my account, I could look at his bill. I had never opened anyone else's mail. But I just had to. I opened it and there was a number that he was calling over and over again. Seventy-two minutes for one call, fifty-four minutes for another. There were twenty-four calls he made to that number. That only said one thing to me; he was cheating.

It was about midnight by the time I opened that envelope. I logged on to my computer and Googled the number. Up popped her picture. She looked a lot like me. So now I had her name. I knew I would wait until morning to call her. At 8:00 a.m. I called her. I told her that I had found her number a couple of times on my cell phone bill, and I just wanted to verify that it wasn't a wrong number. She

hung out. No sex. He helped me through my break up with my fiancé. I cried; he listened. I vented; he offered advice. I talked him through a couple of breakups of his own. It was a wonderful supportive friendship.

About year six of our friendship, my friends started asking me why we weren't dating. I kept saying, "Because he's better than a boyfriend." Then he sat down with me one day and asked me if we could move our friendship to the next level. He said he wanted to try to have a relationship with me. I told him I didn't know if I was willing to lose our friendship if our relationship ended badly. Honestly, that conversation went on for a year. We'd talk about it all the time. My gut told me we'd lose our friendship if we started dating.

Finally I acquiesced. He had built a good case for our friendship being so strong that we couldn't possibly ever lose our connection. So we started dating exclusively. We were a couple. It was odd but natural. I know that makes no sense at all. Things were going pretty well. We finally slept together. That felt strange to me. But we were changing the dynamic of our life together, so I chalked it up to that. Our communication was changing. He didn't seem to be as clear with what he wanted from our relationship as he was when he made such a good case for us to change from being friends to lovers. I tried to pay attention to the details of his wants and needs. He had very specific fetishes that were fun. But I also noted that he seemed to have a lot of shame or guilt around having sex. I figured we'd work through that too. But it made things very difficult for me. I was having my own issues regarding sex after menopause. My body didn't work the same as it did years prior. After seven years of no sex, that was troublesome for me. But we were going to work through all these issues. I did not want to fail at this relationship.

I started noticing that he wasn't very sensitive or helpful when it came to me having a cold or the flu. I could feel myself starting to reassess this whole thing. But I soldiered on. We had been together as a couple for about nine or ten months when he called me a couple of days before my birthday to let me know he had talked to his accountant about marrying me. What? He wanted his accountant to tell him if it would be financially sound to marry me. The odd thing was,

About six months later, he contacted me and asked if I wanted to meet him for breakfast. I thought it would be the perfect opportunity to find out what happened. He really never answered the question about what happened. We talked about trying to rebuild our friendship. That's what I missed the most—our friendship. I SHOULD have listened to my gut. It was screaming not to have a relationship with him, that our friendship was just fine. But he assured me we'd be OK. I believed him. I tried to believe in us, as a couple. We had breakfast a couple more times, and I realized our friendship had suffered too big of a blow. My trust in him was gone.

But because I am who I am, there were lessons to be learned from that relationship. That will be discussed in another chapter.

After several months, Dad and this woman got engaged. They asked all of us what we thought about them just living together without getting married. It was more about their individual social security payments, etcetera. We all gave our blessing to them to not get married. A few months went by, and they set a date to be married. They thought they SHOULD marry because they were from "that era." I asked this woman to join me for lunch so we could have a private talk. I wanted to be completely candid with her. I told her I thought it was great that she and my dad had found each other and were getting married. I wanted them to be happy together. But I didn't know how she was going to fit into my life, other than as a friend. At thirty-seven years old, I wasn't looking for another mother. I told her I may be a "pill" until I figured it out. But as long as she and Dad were happy, all was right with the world. I think she was a bit taken aback but understood where I was coming from.

The wedding plans were set in motion. They got married at a relative's house. It was a beautiful outdoor wedding. One of her sons walked her down the aisle. They said their vows, and my dad cried.

I really don't remember much. I remember there were a lot of bees. We were now officially *The Brady Bunch*. She had three sons; Dad had two daughters. There were spouses and grandkids on both sides, except for me. No kids, no spouse. What a great clan to be family with! Right? Whoa, hold up. Here's the rest of the story, "Paul Harvey."

After they got married, there were a lot of family gatherings—every Jewish holiday, birthdays, anniversaries. I was happy to show up and more than happy to cook and clean up. I was always at these events with a smile on my face, waiting to bond as a family. The thing was, it wasn't happening. It wasn't for my lack of trying. Oh, have I mentioned who one of the "family" members was? One of the "mean girls" from my high school days—one who tormented me daily. But now we were almost forty. Surely things would be different now, right? No, she hadn't changed a bit. That was when I realized why the bonding wasn't happening. For me this was like being in high school all over again. "They" were the "popular kids"; I was the outsider…again.

set tables, set up buffets, clear dishes, rinse dishes, wrap leftovers, anything to keep me from sitting down for long periods of time. I had helped all I could, and a bunch of us sat down at the kitchen table, including me. My dad, his wife, my stepbrother, and his wife and sister–in–law were all sitting there talking. I'm not sure what led the conversation in the direction it took, but I do know I tried to stop it. My stepbrother brought up the subject of who my dad dated before my dad married his mother. I was immediately on alert, but somehow I couldn't move to get up from the table. So my dad started talking about a couple of women he dated. He mentioned this woman who used to be a neighbor of ours. I was surprised. I never knew he went out with her. My stepbrother's next question about this particular woman was, "So did you bone her?" My sight went blurry; my ears started to ring. I was horrified by the question. I looked at my stepbrother and said, "I would rather blow my head off than hear the answer to that question." I looked at both my dad and his wife. They looked uncomfortable. He asked again, "So did you bone her?" And in front of G-d and everyone, my dad started talking about how he had slept with her, gave some details, and laughed as did my stepbrother. My dad's wife didn't seem amused. I got up and left. I cried all the way home. For me it felt like a violation of sorts, more inappropriate behavior. I was sick to my stomach. I started begging out of dinners periodically after that.

Years later I decided to host a combo Rosh Hashanah/anniversary dinner. It was Dad and his wife's tenth anniversary. I thought that I would have a bit more control of inappropriate behavior if I hosted. What was I thinking? I was going to have the dinner in the party room at my apartment building. No one would have to be in my actual apartment. I started planning about three weeks in advance. People started calling, asking if they could help. I delegated items. Everything seemed to be going smoothly until a few days before the dinner. Everyone that said they were going to do something either wanted to change what they were doing or bringing, didn't know if they would be able to show up, or invited extra people. You've heard the term: "Like herding cats?" Well, I have cats. They're easier to deal with. I had ordered a cake for my dad and his wife's anniver-

Hashanah. Now with that call, I felt disrespected, defeated, and angry. With that call, I found my voice and my backbone. I told her how I felt about everyone's behavior, including her phone call. I told her I thought her family was difficult and disrespectful of me. At that point I could honestly say I didn't care if I was at another "family" gathering again.

She became angry and told me I would not be invited to anything again. For some reason, that was fine with me. I told her she would have to explain to my dad why she wasn't going to invite me to be with him. She had spent so much time manipulating me through guilt, through mentioning my mother, through mentioning what family SHOULD be, I had had enough. I figured my dad would step up and tell her it wasn't OK for her to do that. Every gathering we had been at, whenever I was out of my dad's line of sight, I would hear him say, "Where's Roberta?" How was she going to explain that? Good luck.

Nine days after the Rosh Hashanah fiasco my dad called and told me he lost his cell phone. I told him I had an extra one and would bring it over the next morning after Yom Kippur services. The next morning I went over to drop off the phone. I walked in and there was the table already set for the break-the-fast dinner that night. I quietly counted the place settings. There was enough for everyone but me. I sat down with my dad and showed him how to use the phone. He asked if I was coming to break the fast. I told him I wasn't invited and looked straight into his wife's eyes. He looked at her too. He said nothing. Not a question, not a statement…nothing. I even waited another minute…still nothing. So I left. I ended up breaking the fast at my friend's Asian restaurant. So that was the end of me trying to please. Early on I felt that my dad's wife was manipulative. When she was telling my dad he had too much stuff from the house he had with my mom, she would ask him to give it away either to my sister and me or to some organization. I do have to admit my dad was a pack rat but not a hoarder. One day I was at their place, and she took out some items that were my mother's. I didn't want them. I didn't have room for more stuff. She held up a weighted crystal bird and said in a sing-song voice, "You SHOULD take it, it was

This was right around my dad's ninetieth birthday. She was going to throw a big party for him. I'm sure someone would be taking pictures. Sure enough, the day of the party someone took a family photo—Dad and his wife sitting in the front and the rest of us gathered around. I framed that photo and put it on a small table in the hall facing the front door so if and when they came over, it would be the first thing they saw. On the table, it was out of my sightline most of the time. Yes, a little passive-aggressive, I know!

Remember, I was now related (through Dad's marriage) to one of the "mean girls" from K-12th grade. She called and wanted to know if she could borrow some folding chairs and a folding table. I said sure, but she would have to come over and get them. When she walked in, the first thing she saw was that picture. She said, "What is that, a shrine?" I just had to chuckle. I didn't say anything. I just let the question hang in the air.

Let's just face it, my dad married another narcissist. But this one came with her own narcissistic family. Early on each of them seemed to be interested in getting to know my sister and me. But that waned when the novelty wore off for them. My sister wasn't around them much. Me, I just became "the help" again. I was always being asked to do something. Which beats the alternative, I guess. I noticed there was a lot of manipulation from my dad and his wife. In some instances it was easier to do what they wanted me to do. When I'd put my foot down and said "no, thank you," "no, I don't want to," and "no, I don't think so," my life became more difficult due to the pressure or guilt that both of them would lay on me. My dad would just stop trying to change my mind, but his wife didn't take no for an answer. One of her kids said their nickname for her was "The Bulldozer." Fitting, I thought. Another reason I did all these things with them—for them—my dad was ninety. How much longer could this go on? I know that sounds terrible, but it's honest. Why waste time fighting when time was not on my dad's side?

My dad's wife would ask me what it was like growing up with my mom and dad. At first I would just say, "It was difficult at best." She would press me for some details. I finally told her my mom and dad were abusive. After finding that out, she would jokingly say in

shallow. I kissed him on his forehead and said good-bye. My sister kept saying she was so glad to be there with Dad's wife when the nurse told them to go into my dad's room, that he was taking his last breaths.

My stepmother's kids who lived in town started arriving. My sister's best friend arrived. I called my aunt and cousin to let them know. I called the Rabbi's office to let him know. Then the insanity began. My stepbrother started talking as if he were going to make decisions about the service. Then he stopped and said, "Well, I guess that's really up to the daughters." I remember thinking, you think? Next he called the other stepbrothers that lived in Los Angeles, as did a couple of his kids. He put them on speakerphone. I was sure the people in Los Angeles were going to say we're sorry for your loss or something appropriate. Instead they asked when the service was going to be. We told them Monday, January 14. The next statement will blow your mind. One of the brothers said, "Can't you wait until Wednesday when we can get a cheaper fare?"

My vision went blurry; my ears started to ring. My best friend grabbed on to my hand and squeezed it tight. I looked at her. Telepathically we had an entire conversation. They hung up the phone, and the next thing I knew, my dad's wife started barking orders at me. "You have to call the synagogue! You have to make the arrangements!" Ah, I'm "the help" once again, not a member of the immediate grieving family…"the help." Wow. Mind you, none of these orders were being barked at my sister. In fact, my sister said to me later that day, "I don't know why she didn't ask me to call the caterer. I've done it before." The next day I got a call from my dad's wife's best friend, and she said she was going to take care of all of the catering stuff. I thanked her.

Saturday morning we all met at the funeral home. I barely said a word. All the arrangements were made, and I was glad to go home. Sunday we met with the Rabbi at the synagogue. We were all sitting in this big conference room. There were four conference tables pushed together. I found it interesting where we wanted to sit.

In the furthest corner from the entry were my stepmother and stepbrother. In another corner were my sister and her two kids. In

was in charge. He lined us all up to walk into the sanctuary. We were seated in the pews, and the music started. A few prayers were said, and the Rabbi called me up to give the eulogy. I had asked him to put his hand on my back if I started to shake. I knew that the service was being recorded, both sound and video. I was very calm. I looked up from the podium, and there were a lot of people there. I noticed two of my friends sitting on opposite sides of the sanctuary. I remember thinking, too bad they didn't see each other when they came in. I looked at my best friend. She nodded and gave me a sly smile. I started the eulogy. Somewhere in the middle of it, I looked over at my sister, and she was grinning like a Cheshire cat. Odd, I thought. My dad's wife was staring at me. I couldn't tell what her expression was. I got done, turned around, and hugged the Rabbi. I quietly whispered in his ear in a sing-song way, "Nah, nah, nah, nah, nah, nah." Of course referring to the "oh no you won't" by my dad's wife said the day before. I went back to my seat and felt nothing but relief. A friend of my dad's presented my dad's wife with a folded flag, being they were both members of the Jewish Veteran's organization. It was quite touching. The grand send off for my dad was performed by a pretty well-known singer who stood up and sang Frank Sinatra's "My Way." It was perfect! Because my dad wanted to be cremated, there was no graveside service. We had planned that for spring.

We adjourned downstairs to a social room, had a light lunch, and talked to everyone. All of this was almost over. Usually Shiva is one week long. My dad didn't want that. So we planned it for one night—that night at the synagogue. My best friend and I went back to my house. We had to be back around six. The last part of the worst of it...so I thought.

My dad's wife decided my sister, and I had to come over to the condo for the next two days to go through all of my dad's stuff. There was so much crap to sort through! Old bills, old files, work stuff, stuff that was his and my mom's. There was an old Xerox machine that he insisted on keeping, books, tons of papers, birth certificates for himself and my mom, all stuffed in boxes, in drawers, and on shelves. It seemed endless. At one time during this cleaning, my sister and Dad's wife ended up in the kitchen together. They were speaking quietly to

was. As far as I knew, my ninety-four-year-old father had outlived his money, and I was right. There were several insurance policies, including one that my mom was beneficiary. She had been dead for eighteen years at that point. So this would now include finding a death certificate for my mom, which I found in a box of papers the day before. What made this even more insane, it wasn't even a significant amount of money. I was portrayed and treated so badly for what? This? It was enough to pay the next year's estimated taxes, buy myself a Galaxy Tablet, and move from the awful place I was living. When it was all said and done, the executor decided to release all funds to me because I had turned fifty-four in December, and it was now April. I was devastated by the wording in the will. It cut me off at the knees. I cried for months. Who did my dad think I was? Why didn't he want to know me? I, obviously, was just "the help."

While all this mess was going on, my dad's wife/widow was continuing to call and bully me. Her manipulations weren't working anymore. I was saying no to her emphatically. She had called my aunt in Chicago and said something unflattering about me. A switch flipped for me that day. I had had enough! I called my dad's wife and for lack of a better term, "broke up" with her in April 2013. I told her I was glad she made my dad happy. But to me she was nothing more than a manipulative bully. She said, "No one has ever called me a bully before." The smart-ass part of me thought, well, someone evidently had called her manipulative before. She was stunned. I told her I owed her nothing. But I wasn't going to be treated like "the help" anymore—that she had her own biological children who could cater to her. I told her I didn't want to communicate with her anymore. She said, "Well, if you don't want a family." I countered with, "Don't you understand? I never had one." And she said, "Well, OK," and hung up. I hadn't spoken to her since then until I ran into her at a local Target store. I was cordial, asked how she was, listened, and then said I had to go. That was February 2014. I haven't seen or spoken to her since. It does feel like a huge burden has been lifted off my shoulders. I finally feel like I have some peace of mind.

In July 2014 there was an event at the synagogue for my friend the Rabbi. It was his twenty-fifth anniversary of being in the

CHAPTER 11

Family of Choice

Let me tell you about my real family, my family of choice. We are bonded to each other, we don't judge each other, and we are there for each other. Isn't that what a true family SHOULD be like?

Tricia: My best friend is who I dedicated this book to. She has been my best friend since we met in our tenth-grade art class. She was sitting by herself, looking so sad. I felt drawn (excuse the pun) to her. I sat down next to her, and we started to talk. It was such a natural thing. We started to spend a lot of time together. We even shared lockers. The first time I slept over at her house, we got into this big bed together. She had a king-sized mattress on the floor. We finally fell asleep after talking a lot. Somewhere in the middle of the night, she had rolled over and wrapped herself around me. She was sound asleep; I was startled and afraid to move. I didn't want to wake her up. But this was a first for me. She eventually rolled over to the other side of the bed. I talked to her about it in the morning. She said, "Yeah, I do that. I'm sorry." I told her no problem. Nothing like that would make any difference to me. She

about not letting "boys" get in the way of our friendship. We talked everything out, and as if no time had passed, we went on with our best friendship. Even with our two "boy" bumps in the road, our friendship could not be torn apart. We made a fresh start. I don't know what I would've done without her then or now. We both know that listening is key. We don't necessarily need each other to fix what's going on, we just need to be good listeners. We've been through hell and high water together. We agree that sometimes friends feel helpless, especially during a parent's illness and death. We also feel helpless when we see each other in bad relationships. We just have to ride the wave and hold on. She is my most important relationship. It's a healthy, loving, respectful one. Our relationship is fun loving, and we can communicate with no words at all. The way it SHOULD be.

Glenda: Another family of choice is a girlfriend I met in junior high. We were so close. I spent a lot of time at her house. We even played cards with her mom and grandma. I loved being there. Everyone seemed to love each other the way they SHOULD. They enjoyed each other's company. They liked having me around. She and I laughed a lot. We sang together, we were in choir together. We even tried out for the school talent show together. We sang "Top of the World" by the Carpenters and one other song. We didn't get selected to be in the talent show. We were a little disappointed, but that was OK with us. I still have that sheet music. I have the notes we passed in class too. They are still folded up in a football shape. She came over many years ago, and we opened and read them all. She said about herself, "Boy, was I bossy." I said, "Yes, you were. But that was OK with me." I loved her no matter what, and still do. We try to see each other once a month. It doesn't always happen, but we do play catch-up via the phone.

We lost touch during high school. We would see each other in the hall but didn't have any classes together. After

December and welcome them to it in March. It's always a fun get-together. Over the almost forty years we've known each other, we've realized no one wants material gifts. We want the gift of time to be together to laugh, to share a meal, and share stories…whatever. We also agree, how much material crap do we need?

Even through my bad relationships, my family problems, my agoraphobia, and anxiety disorder, these three women have been rocks for me. July 13 to 15, 2014, I took my first vacation in almost twenty years. Tricia and I drove up to Glenda's lake home. I couldn't believe I was considering it, let alone driving two and a half hours away from everything familiar and comfortable. With all of their support and no pressure, I drove 145 miles away from my home. What an accomplishment! My best friend is the best copilot there is. She knows just how much information to give me and how to deliver it. She read the directions while I drove. I can honestly say I only had a couple bouts of temporary anxiety. My therapist has always told me there's a thin line between anxiety and excitement. Both are adrenaline based. So I just remembered that while I drove. I even texted him when we stopped for breakfast. He texted back, "Congratulations. Now you can plan your trip to California." To which I replied, "One trip at a time, please."

I called Glenda from the road to let her know where we were. Oddly, there was no answer. I figured because she's really not a morning person, she was sleeping. Tricia and I are the "crack of cock-a-doodle-doo" girls. We stopped for breakfast and after we ate I called again. No answer. Strange. I left a message for her. When we got back in the car, she called back. She apologized. She saw that she missed five calls, not all were mine. She said she had her music up really loud and was singing and didn't hear her phone. I told her I had just said, "Well, this will suck if we get there and she's not there." Of course causing Tricia

But he was the nicest cat I've ever had. He was protective, like a "watch cat."

I've moved a couple of times, and we've never lost touch. We've had some pretty heavy differences over the years, but it's never stopped us from being friends. As we get older, our bond gets stronger. I couldn't ask for someone to be more in my corner at this stage in my life. She worries about dementia due to her family history, and I've promised to visit her in "the home" and reintroduce myself on a daily basis. She calls me a smart-ass and laughs.

Elaine: Another family of choice I kiddingly call "Jesus." She is the most level-headed woman, so together. She's kind, reliable, honest...wait, I'm making her out to sound like a girl scout (or a German shepherd). She's not. But she would do anything to help her friends. I met her at the bank I had my account at. If she knew I was having financial trouble, she would sneak deposits into my account. I asked her not to, but she did it anyway. That stinker! I loved her for that and so many other reasons. I love her for including me at her family dinners. I've spent two Thanksgivings with her family. It's such a warm and lovely place to be. So unlike all my "family" get-togethers. My favorite gatherings were all the Christmas Eves I was included in. I called myself their "token Jew." Funniest part of the whole thing, I knew more Christmas carols than they did! All those years in choir paid off for something. It was like a *Saturday Night Live* sketch.

Beth: She's my funniest friend who can make me laugh no matter what. We met when I was a manicurist. She came into the salon I was working in and heard me talking about a local concert I wanted to go to, but the tickets were sold out. She said to me, "My husband and I have two extra tickets. Do you want to go with us?" And so a friendship was formed. We've been through so much together. We are no longer married to "those husbands" anymore. Our goal, as I see it, is to find the absurdity in life and make fun

CHAPTER 12

"Aha Moments"
Movies, Books, Magazine
Articles, and Conversations

I've always been fascinated by autobiographies and biographies. I think it's because I like to see what people have been through to get to where they are today. In most of those books the writers have had one thing in common—resilience. If you ask my friends, they would agree I have that quality as well. My therapist would say the same. I've even said, "I'm so sick of sticking my hand in the resiliency bucket I could throw up."

I've been lucky enough to have the same therapist on and off for the last thirty-one years. That's a really long time not to be able to bullshit your way through anything. Not that I would even try. I trust him implicitly. Just a few weeks ago I was telling him that at age twenty-one I was planning on killing myself. Everything just seemed to be too much for me. So I went to the Humane Society to say good-bye to the animals, and then I was going to slam my car into a bridge. Guess what! A small, lonely kitten grabbed onto my ankle and wouldn't let go. No matter what I did, she wouldn't let me go. I ended up adopting that five-week-old runt of a kitten. I walked

sounds, why is that so hard? I know that in my past I have given too many chances to people, whether they're family or relationships. The relationships include friendships as well as boyfriends. When I started letting those lessons of Maya Angelou sink in, things began to shift for me, a little bit at first, more so later.

My then husband and I joined a different synagogue than my parents. We were at Rosh Hashanah services, and the sermon the Rabbi was giving was about when life begins, abortion, and personhood. He said, "Life may begin at conception, but personhood begins at birth." What an epiphany! I realized I could forgive myself for the abortion I had in high school. We left the synagogue and went right over to my parents' house. At sixteen, I was too afraid of what they would do to me if they knew I was pregnant. I had kept this deep, dark secret from them for years. It was time to tell them and unburden myself of that secret. The oddest thing happened. My mother asked me who the "daddy" was. If she would have stopped and thought about it, it could have only been one person. Before I could answer, my father said, "It's none of your business." Wow! Not what I expected at all. But it was a giant weight lifted off my twenty-eight-year-old shoulders.

I have spent a lifetime trying to learn about myself. I've been in therapy; I've read a lot of psychology books. I've watched self-help seminars and TV shows. One of the most helpful was an Oprah show in the late eighties and early nineties. I think it was John Bradshaw. He was talking about taking your inner child by the hand and walking her/him away from the pain of growing up in a dysfunctional home. What a wonderful exercise! So I visualized taking my young self by the hand and walking down the hill from the cul-de-sac we lived on. For all the times I was told to go play on the highway near our house, I visualized taking my inner child down the road that led to the highway to remind my inner child it was not safe to play on the highway and not fair or nice to be told to go play on the highway. That was twenty-plus years ago, and I remember it as clearly as yesterday. I cried a big cleansing cry.

show and its search for missing family members with outcomes both good and bad, but I got totally hooked. It has seemed to open up a can of worms for me. I cry out of joy when families are reunited. I cry bitter tears for family members that are abandoned with no explanation why. All of these tears make me think how nice it would have been to have a functional family. How I would prefer I was speaking with my sister now that our parents are gone. How an explanation or an apology may (or may not) help. But there is no resolution—let me rephrase, the resolution for me is to keep my distance from the toxicity that is my relationship with my sister. Sad but true.

Do you think if I told Troy about my crazy-ass family, he would find me a family I could love and would love me and appreciate me for who I am?

I have read:

> Malcolm Gladwell's *Blink*
> Ted Zeff's *The Highly Sensitive Person*
> John Edwards' *If G-d Were the Sun*
> Claire Weekes' *Hope and Help for Your Nerves*

I've read so many others, I can't even remember the names of them. I was trying to understand what was "wrong" with me. My parents and my sister told me all the time there was something wrong with me. It must be true, right? Meanwhile, my parents told my aunt and uncle in Chicago that I was a difficult child. They told them that I misbehaved and caused trouble all of the time. Of course I didn't find this out until a few years ago. I don't know why they would think I was bad, difficult, stupid, careless, and lazy. I was never any of those things. I certainly had my own ideas and opinions. But as you grow up, isn't that what SHOULD happen? As long as you're not hurting anyone with your personal beliefs, you SHOULD be entitled to those beliefs, right?

As I was contemplating writing my autobiography, I read a review in my local newspaper about a book called *Family Trouble* by Joy Castro. http://www.joycastro.com/FamilyTrouble.htm

CHAPTER 13

What I Know For Sure
(This should be a short chapter)

My life is more like a Tyler Perry movie than Rodgers and Hammerstein.

Minimizing what has happened in my life does not make it OK, less upsetting, or less scary.

Trust your gut. Trust your truth.

A kitten saved my life.

There's a difference between a sense of duty and "SHOULDING."

After being told my whole life that there was something wrong with me, I now know I'm the healthy one. Go figure!

Clichés I hate:

Making lemonade from lemons. Sometimes lemons are just that... lemons.

Play with the cards you're dealt. But sometimes the cards are stacked against you, and you have to play anyway.

I have been thinking about donating my brain to science, like the football players are doing. It would be interesting to find out

parents viewed telling me they would pay for a nose job as taking care of me. How things "looked" to others was most important to them.

Maybe it was naïveté that made me want to trust my parents. Regardless of what was going on, you SHOULD be able to trust your parents, right? Trust and safety go hand in hand. So I SHOULD be safe too. But I wasn't safe…ever. I don't think I understood that. I wanted to trust them. So every time something would happen, I would put it in the back of my mind. I was SHOULDING myself. How I thought things SHOULD be. If wishing could have only made it so.

Once I had a better understanding of what would set everyone off, I would try so hard not to do that. The problem with that, what set everyone off changed daily, so you wouldn't have any scenario to use as a constant. There was no way to stay out of harm's way. It was so frustrating.

I'm sure it's shocking to hear I have trust issues. I trust my closest friends implicitly. But any farther than that, not so much.

I want to believe that people are inherently good. But people keep proving me wrong. At fifty-six, that's OK. I have my closest core group of friends. They accept me for who I am. Those are the people I SHOULD trust. I've worked hard on those relationships. They are the most important people in my life.

You can't be everything to everybody. No matter how hard you try. You need to be true to yourself. That is one of the lessons I had to learn. Another lesson is you can't hold other people to the standard you hold yourself to.

Facing your fears is not a bad thing. With experience SHOULD come the power of knowledge.

This resiliency of mine got me to where I am today. It bonded me to lifelong friendships, which are better than blood relatives.

The most important lesson I've learned: I choose me. Not in a narcissistic way, but in a healthy, empowered way.

I've thought a lot about how to end this book. If I want to continue to be my authentic self, I have to end it three different ways.

ABOUT THE AUTHOR

Roberta Brown was born and raised in a suburb of Minneapolis, Minnesota. She has always written, whether it was in journals, short stories in writing classes in high school, or business letters with a clever twist. Roberta's obsession with Cher and Cher's nails led her to go to cosmetology school and get her manicuring license. After being in the beauty business for twenty years, an anxiety disorder forced her to change direction. Roberta reinvented herself and started her own business as a marketing consultant and client-services director working from home. That business is small and going strong to this day. *THE SHOULDING A Story of Resilience and Hope* is her first book. Roberta continues to live in the Minneapolis area with her cats, better known as her "fuzzy children."

www.ingramcontent.com/pod-product-compliance
Lightning Source LLC
LaVergne TN
LVHW051757080426

835511LV00018B/3337